To Joy best

Brown Edge
Memories 2

Hedgelaying at Greenway Bank Farm, c1940. Joseph Haydon is 4th left and John Bailey Snr is 2nd left.

Compiled by Elizabeth Lawton

Front cover: St Anne's Church Queen, Barbara Heath, on School Bank, 1950.
On the right of float, Margaret Pointon, Mary Holdcroft and Irene Shallcross.
Back cover: Top - Alan Hancock left and his brother, Ivan right, visit American army camp.
Middle - Stefan Staszko, centre, with friends.
Bottom - A good time at Blackpool c1928.
L-R: ? Sheldon, Daniel Durber, William Berrisford, Jack Turner, ?, George Davenport.

CHURNET VALLEY BOOKS
1 King Street, Leek, Staffordshire. ST13 5NW 01538 399033
www.leekbooks.co.uk
© Elizabeth Lawton and Churnet Valley Books 2008
ISBN 9781904546610

Knypersley Mill Farm, early 1950s.
L-R: TH Holdcroft, R Yardley, Mrs I Holdcroft, Mrs ME Yardley. Jack Holdcroft on the hay and the horse 'Bella'.

A drawing of St Anne's School, looking down from Chapel Lane. Drawn by Stanford Charlesworth in 1954.

Contents

I would like to thank all the many people who have contributed to this book.
I apologise for any errors.

Elsie Charlesworth's retirement as a dinner lady at St Anne's School c1974. The vicar is Rev A Moseley.

Mary Ellis née Willis

I was born in 1943 at Top Chapel Lane. It was called Foster's Row before that, by the locals mainly, because all my Foster ancestors lived there and they were a very big family. There were four brothers - my grandfather, Jack Foster, and Tom who was Ted Foster's father. Then there was Frank and George and they all had houses in Top Chapel Lane. My grandparents were in No 6 which is now called Hunter's Cottage.

Grandma's name was Jane Pickford before she was married. Grandad Jack and his brother Tom married two sisters from Leek. They were Nellie and Jane but were usually called Ellen and Ginny. My mother was Lily Foster and my dad, Vincent Willis, came from Brindley Ford.

Grandfather bought the cottage as a one up and one down but he was a stonemason and was always fetching stone from Marshes Hill, with a wheelbarrow. The cottage ended up with three bedrooms and three rooms downstairs, including a front parlour and a passageway in between.

I was actually born at number six but my mother and dad used to live next door but one.

Mary's grandfather, Jack Foster, outside his cottage in Top Chapel Lane c1934 with his grandson Frank.

They rented a little old cottage off Eber Charlesworth but we went back to live at Grandma's, No 6, when I was about twelve, because she was on her own then.

We had a marvellous childhood - I can't tell you - we had good parents, and I had four brothers, Alan, John, Peter and Roy and there was never a dull moment.

I think I was about four when they dug the holes for the two pylons (there's only one now). I was a nuisance to my brother Alan, because everywhere he went he had to take me with him. Even from a little girl he used to swear me to secrecy, that I didn't tell Mother and Dad what him and his friends had been up to. Anyway they dug these holes for the pylons and it was all clay, sheer clay, I must have got on his nerves this particular day and him and his mate lowered me down the bottom of the hole and left me. The holes were almost as high as a house.

I remember sitting down the bottom of this hole and Bert Pye came. He was uncle to Edwin Sims and lived up Lask Edge on a farm. He used to ride a bike. He'd be about twelve or thirteen. How he knew I was down that hole I'll never know, because his hearing was bad. Anyway he came and looked over and got me out. From that day I was big mates with Bert. He was a great fellow - a smashing man.

We were always across Marshes Hill and down Knypersley and the feeder - we just had our freedom - but my brother was always with me. We were never without a dog either.

One of my earliest memories was the 1947 snow when I was about four. The old lady

Fred Foster c1958. (Mary's mother's half-brother).

Mary's mother, Lily Willis, née Foster. (b. 1918 d. 1996).

Lily Foster and her brother Ambrose c1926.

Mum and Dad's wedding, Vincent and Lily Willis.
c1938, outside Hunter's Lodge.

down at Lions Paw Wood died, and they were a long time before they buried her, because they couldn't dig the ground in the churchyard. I think her name was Beech but I'm not 100% sure. Anyway when they eventually did bury her everybody then used to turn out for a funeral. We always used to stand at the end of the lane when a funeral went past, and the old men used to doff their hats. Anyway she went past and they'd brought her on a sledge - they couldn't get any other transport through.

My dad was in Africa when I was born. He was in the army and I think I was about six months old before my dad actually saw me. He was amongst the first to go when the call up came for the army. One pet hate of Dad's was conscientious objectors. I always remember walking over School

ABOVE: Mary's dad, Vincent Willis, with pit ponies from Whitfield. Dad on the left, Arthur Lovatt on the right.

LEFT: Group of miners at Whitfield. Fred Foster, Lily's half-brother 2nd from the right.

Miners. Dad 1st left.

Bank when I was little and saying 'Good morning Mr Conchie' to this gentleman and he said, 'What did you call me Mary?' I said 'Mr Conchie' and he went berserk with me. I went home and told me dad I'd seen Mr Conchie on School Bank and he'd gone mad with me. My father laughed and almost fell off the chair he was on. It was Dad's name for him and I thought it was his real name.

Dad was shot in the foot in the war. When he came home from the

war Judith Sheldon's mother was standing at her gate and she couldn't believe it was him. He was a wreck. He was twelve stone something when he went and he was six when he came back. Before he went to war he was a very good Methodist and he came back a non-believer.

He always worked at Whitfield. He worked with the horses, with Arthur Lovatt from Lask Edge. Arthur was like the top man with the horses and my dad always worked with him. Dad died at 64. He was made redundant at 58 from Whitfield and had a bad back. All the time he was working we never knew him to have a day off work only New Year's Day - seven days a week. He was a real hard worker - it was just work and bed. When he came home we'd be lined up to give him a kiss before bed. We just never really got to know him. He was very Victorian but quiet and shy in a lot of ways. He gave me a hard time when I was a teenager. He was up at four o'clock every morning - if he was up we were up. I think that's why now I love to lie in bed.

I used to feel very put on because being the only girl I had to clean up and get the veg ready - you had to do a bucketful. There was Gran, me, Mum and Dad and four brothers - Imagine ironing shirts for five men - it was hard work.

Dad was always larger than life. If he told you to do something you did it - you didn't argue. He just looked at you and you knew you'd get a back-hander. Even today I still don't believe that a smack does a child any harm - there's a big difference between a smack and abuse.

Animals - I can't tell you - we've had everything. My dad was animal mad. We

Top Chapel Lane. Back L-R: Gladys and Lily Foster (Mary's mother).

had a peacock and peahen, always had banties, pigeons, and canaries - them were the norm. We had grass snakes, a crow and a sparrowhawk they were training. As we got a bit better off we used to rear half a dozen turkeys from June until Christmas. By the time Christmas came they were thirty-six pound each. We used to be up to the eyes in down when we used to pluck these turkeys. Everything was homemade at Christmas - we even made our own streamers.

We were poor like everybody else but we never went hungry - Dad was a good provider. Ray Holdcroft's dad was always shooting rabbits and hares. We'd always got rabbits on the go. One night I came home from work and opened the pantry door and this hare six foot long was hanging on the back of it. As I opened the door it hit me in the face - oh we had some fun, we really did.

I was reared with the fact that when someone died you went and looked at them. My first memory of that was when we all went to the Free Mission. Mary Davenport, who lived in one of the cottages at Hill Top, died when she was seven. I was younger than that but I can remember ever so clearly going in the hallway and looking at her in this little coffin. They don't do that today do they?

We had to go to the Free Mission three times every Sunday, 11 o'clock, then 2 o'clock Sunday school, then evening service at 6 o'clock. The three Charlesworth brothers ran it - Jack, Wilfred and Eber, just these old men and us kids and we used to laugh - we were very

Ready to go on stage at the chapel, c1951.
L-R: David Willis, Elaine Jervis, Mary, John Willis,
Maureen Foster.

BELOW: Mary's cousin, Elaine Jervis, as Sandy Lane
Chapel queen c1959.
Back L-R: Mrs Ada Jervis, Elaine Jervis.
3rd row: Marie Pepper, ?, Derek Bate, Susan Baker.
Front: ?, Mary Ellis, Gillian Wedgwood.

BELOW:
Mr Brown's class St. Anne's late 1950s.
Back L-R: Brian Gilman, Philip
Hodgkinson, Roy Mitcheson, Russell
Lambsdale, Adrian Mickiewicz, Peter Willis,
Leon Fielding, Terry Slater, John Holloway.

Seated: Jill Sherratt, Susan ?, Jean Bartlem,
Judith Berrisford, Mr Brown, Julia Tyler,
June Bourne, Shirley Simcock, Agnes Rob,
Hilary Mathews.

Front: John Clews, Dave Snape,
Julian Kirta, Brian Banner.

rude. They kept saying 'Alleluia' 'The Lord be praised' and 'God Bless' all the way through the service, we couldn't stop giggling. We used to go through the top pub yard to get to the Mission and one day Eber Charlesworth got hold of me and said *'Dare to be a Daniel, dare to stand alone - dare to pass a public house and take your money home.'* We laughed about it but I've always remembered it.

There was a chap called Dick Cudd and where he came from I don't know. I always thought he was a tramp. There was a family at the end of the lane called Rowley and Dick used to come and stop in their pig cote at the back of the house. As kids we used to sit and talk to him. He looked rough but there was no harm in him. Bill Worthy was another character. He went round with his goat on a rope. He lived under Marshes Hill, the first place on the left after Judgefields. He was a lovely man. We were always with him as kids.

We all wore clogs at home. The lads wore old black clogs with tips on. My father was always falling out with me eldest brother cause he'd never got any tips on and they'd get worn out. We thank God he didn't though. We used to play cowboys and Indians in the field behind. My brother scaled a thin metal pole, where the chap next door had been doing some DIY electrics. The electricity went straight through him and it actually held him to the pole. It burnt all his hands, but it didn't kill him, because as it went down to his feet and hit the bottom of his clogs it released him. If he'd had tips on it would have killed him.

I think Grandad Foster died in 1945, I was only about two. My mother used to tell me that every time they came home from work they never knew what he'd do next to the house. They'd got a mixed family, three brothers and two sisters and had a great big open bedroom. The Rose and Crown had had some partitioning taken down. It had Parker's Ales, Double Diamond works wonders and all this on. Well they came home one night and this partitioning was across the bedroom. My Auntie Ada was very religious. She married Jack Charlesworth later in life. She said, 'If you think I'm sleeping under Parker's Ales, Double Diamond works wonders you can think again!' Grandad, no more ado, went upstairs and with a great big sledgehammer smashed it all up. For months after they had to have a roll of wallpaper on string that parted the lads and the girls. Grandad refused to put another wall in.

In them days they always had to wash in the kitchen, at the sink. They had the bath on the hearth when the miners came home. My mother had got three brothers and father, all miners, and they all used to come home in their dirt.

Mother worked at Brough and Nicholson at Leek, in the mills, when she was fourteen. When she had us, to make ends meet, she used to go out and clean a bit. Mother had a great sense of humour - she was a killer. She came to live with us for the last thirteen years of her life and we never had a miss word. She was 78 when she died.

Note:

Mary's memory was very good. I checked the Brown Edge church burial registers and found an entry for Mary Ann Beech, Lion's Paw Farm, who died 5th March 1947 aged 71 years.

After the publication of my last book, *Brown Edge Memories,* Mary rang me to say how much she was enjoying it, and she told me of so many of her memories. I said I would have to tape her story, which is what I did, in October 2006, having no plans for another book at the time. I am so glad that I did as Mary was well at the time but later her health deteriorated. Sadly she died in May 2008, after a brave fight against her illness. I always intended her to be the first one in this book. She loved her village and will always be remembered.

Eric Rowland

I was born in 1945 at Steinfields' Cottages, Broad Lane. I was the second child to Elsie and John Rowland. A sister, Beryl, died three or four years before I was born. She was only four and a half when she died, of meningitis. I have a younger sister, Joan. Mum has lived at Steinfields since she was married and she is now 93.

My mother's name was Elsie Biddulph before she was married. She was born at Rock End, Biddulph Moor and was the eldest of five children. There was Elsie, Harold, William, Francis and Vincent. Grandma and Grandad, George and Ethel Biddulph moved eventually to St.Luke's Mission, Hill Top. They lived in the cottage attached, and were caretakers and cleaners to the mission. Hill Top was in Endon parish then and Mr Heaton had the mission built in 1900, so that the parishioners wouldn't have to walk to Endon Church. The first caretaker was Mr Isaac Harvey, my great grandfather.

Dad came from Sheldon's Row, Norton Green. He was one of four - three girls and a boy. His parents were Frederick Cliff and Elizabeth Emma Rowland. There's only Alice left now, Dad's sister, in Rock Cottage Nursing Home and 91.

Dad always worked at Whitfield but he didn't work on the coalface. He worked on top as a banksman, then with the powder magazine. The powder was for the explosives used in the mine, and was kept in a separate building for obvious reasons. Dad used

Alice Rowland and friends on her 80th birthday. Standing L-R: Roy Cotterill, Ken Elden, Ivy Painter, Charlie Barker, Carol Bradbury, Pam Clarke, Reg Halfpenny, June Cotterill. Seated: Helen Cope, Annie Shallcross, Betty Painter, Elaine Machin, Beryl Halfpenny, Judith Hodgkinson, ?. Front: Alice, Rita Elden.

to walk through the fields, as a lot of them did. Occasionally they went on bikes down Tongue Lane, and odd times they went on Turner's bus from School Bank. He had a car when I was about ten and the car took over. All he said was he didn't want me working in the Pit. Grandad Biddulph worked at Whitfield as well.

When I was little, at Steinfields, Sam Sheldon lived in the farm opposite, and his mum and dad lived in the little cottage across from the farm. Next door to us was George and Alice Mayer. George was a signalman at Endon Station. Before that he used to run two service buses which he later sold to Brown's bus company.

I only went occasionally to St.Luke's Mission on Sunday nights. I usually went to the Free Mission, Charlesworth's Mission, morning and afternoon. When we got a little bit older, and a bit more interested in the opposite sex, there was more attraction at Hill Top Methodist Church. It was more fun over there. We used to go to the youth club and play subuteo, snooker and table tennis. We also played five-a-side football on the tennis court there - that was good. We used to have matches occasionally with other chapels within the circuit. We listened to music but I don't think we did much dancing. Roy Cottrell was involved with it and John Mountford and Wallis Turner.

ABOVE: Eric's mum and dad on their
wedding day August 1937.
L-R: Alice Rowland, Harold Biddulph, John
Rowland, Elsie Rowland, George Biddulph,
Francis Biddulph.

St. Luke's Mission, Hill Top
(also known as Harvey's Mission)

BELOW:
Eric and sister Joan, at Steinfields

I went to Brown Edge Infant's School with Mrs Powditch and then I went to the big school. Mr Fisher was headmaster then. Mrs Proctor taught there and Arthur Berrrisford (Freda's husband). I can't remember the others - must have made a big impression! Mrs Mosedale (Betty Jolley) taught me at one time.

I passed my eleven-plus and went to Leek High School. There were six or seven that passed that year. The girls went to Westwood Hall at Leek. We used to go to school, at Leek, on the P.M.T. bus from Brown Edge. I was fit then. I used to run down most mornings and stagger back up the bank at night. There was quite a crowd of us used to walk up. There was Dave and Linda Harvey, Kathleen Cumberlidge, Shirley Brassington and Marion Lomas. We used to have a good laugh - good times. We were Hill Toppers and we never joined Sandy Laners or School Bankers until we were older.

I didn't do particularly well at Leek High School. I left in 1961 and started work at Leek railway station. The station was where Morrisons is now. I worked down the Churnet Valley line as a booking and parcels office clerk. They used to have three passenger trains a day when I was there, three out and two in. It was used a lot for the Thomas Bolton factory, Uttoxeter to Leek. I booked tickets at odd occasions at Endon station. I also worked at Cheddleton station, mainly dealing with Brittain's traffic. Then Dr Beeching came along, cut the trains, and that was that.

I've been a Port Vale fan all my life. Grandad Biddulph used to give me 1/6d a week to wash his backyard. I used to go from Hill Top to Port Vale on the bus, go in, and have change out of that 1/6d. From when I was about nine or ten I went to the Vale, every home match, and have done so ever since. Lots of lads from Brown Edge School went as well.

We started going to the T.A.B. in St Anne's Vale as we got a bit older. I was never a member but I used to go to the Thursday night dance, as it was called. Arthur Sherratt used to sit there with his drum and playing records. There was a lot there dancing - it was good. A lot of girls from Westwood went there. I did me bit - jiving. There never used to be any trouble and it used to finish early - about half past ten. There was no alcohol in there - just soft drinks. Anyone who wanted alcohol had to sneak out and go to the top pub.

We went on family holidays from the year dot. We went to Colwyn Bay for years and years. It was the highlight of the year. As we had no car we used to go with Herbert Bourne's taxi and used to pick another family up at Ball Green. It was Dave Wright's family. We used to go for a week, in August, to the same place - Mrs Hall's boarding house. Bourne's taxi was driven by Eric Hargreaves who used to live in Church Road. I have photos of Dad on the beach, in his collar and tie, as they all did.

After the TAB I started socializing in Leek. I remember going to Leek Town Hall and all the live bands went there. The Rolling Stones were there on Christmas Eve, before they made the big time. I think it was about

Eric on holiday at Colwyn Bay.

10/6d to go in to see them. The Searchers came as well and The Hollies were quite regular. It used to be packed to the doors. There was not much trouble, and if there was, it was soon sorted out. It was soft drinks only again. If you wanted alcohol you had to have a pass out, and if you had too much they wouldn't let you back in again

The last bus back was about a quarter past ten, which was far too early. We used to walk from Leek to home in an hour. There'd be about four to six of us walking together. Once you got to the Wheel pub it went dark, with no street lights, until you reached The Black Horse. We'd get lifts occasionally.

I left Hill Top when I married my wife, Jill, but we have now returned and absolutely love it. Ken Turner had our present house built about forty years ago. The land was part of Mrs Dawson's garden (Grace Hewitt's mother) at Mission Cottage. I am once again a Hill Topper!

When I was at St Anne's School I did a project on Brown Edge called 'Brown Edge in the 1950s'. I thought it might be of interest to include some extracts from it.

BROWN EDGE IN THE 1950S

Houses: There are about 500 houses. Most of them are brick built but there are a lot of stone houses. The stone was quarried locally and is a hard brown sandstone, called millstone grit. Since 1945 about 50 brick houses have been built and the National Coal Board have built about 90 Cornish type houses.

Michael Bourne, a boy in my class, remembers when he used to live at Bluestone Cottages and he had to go up a ladder to bed. The ladder was fixed to a hole in the ceiling.

There are five springs and wells. They are situated at Woodhouse Lane, Sytch Road, Sandy Lane, one opposite the Foaming Quart, and Star well at Hill Top. Anthony Slater in my class fetches five buckets of water a day from Sandy Lane spout, and pours them into a pitcher tub. He is the only boy in my class who has not got tap water.

List of shops:

Simcock - grocery	Paddock - drapery	Jolley - grocery
Crossley - cakes	Dawson - cobbler	Moore - hairdresser
Shawcross - wool	Powell - petrol & bicycles	Johnson - grocery
Bratt - butchers	Jones - cobbler	Harrison - butchers
Bourne - petrol & repairs Oakes - petrol & repairs		Tyler - grocery & hardware
Berrisford - grocery & vegetables	Sherratt - newspapers & stationary	
Winkle - post office & general	Cumberlidge - grocery & vegetable	
Garner - ladies hairdresser & grocery	Co-op - general store & butchers	
Berrisford - fish & chips & green grocery	Charlesworth - sweets & hardware	

There are about 23 shops. There are four shops supplied by ice-cream firms; Mr Simcock is supplied by Meadow Cream, Mr Cumberlidge sells Lyons, Mr Sherratt sells Walls and Mrs Johnson also sells Lyons. A few shops sell groceries but also a few other things. Mrs Jolley sells some patent medicines and Mrs Johnson keeps a few clothing articles.

The Co-op has separate counters selling meat, grocery and cakes, and bits of hardware. Mrs Crossley bakes cakes in the village but roundsmen belonging to Boyce Adams, Swettenhams, Bowcocks, Mother's Pride, Embreys and the Co-op, bring bread into the village. There are three butchers; Harrisons and Bratts kill their own meat but Co-op meat comes from their own slaughterhouses in the Potteries.

People still fetch their own milk from farms owned by Mr Jesse Sheldon, Mr Shufflebottom and Mr Sam Sheldon, but most of the farmers put their milk on the milk wagon. Mr Clements has a milk round in the village as does Mr Adams and his son, Joe. Mr Weaver and the Co-op also bring milk into Brown Edge.

If you need a new bicycle you could either go to town or order one at Mr Powell's garage, or at Mr Oakes, at Hill Top. Mr Turner mends radios. The travelling hardware vans come selling their goods. These belong to Mr Taylor from Norton, Frosts of Milton and Boyce Adams. People are glad when these vans come, as they are able to buy brushes, bowls, soap and soapflakes.

Brown Edge Post Office is in High Lane and is kept by Mr Winkle. It is not a telegraph office. If you want to send a telegram it is telephoned through to Stockton Brook telegraph office. When telegrams arrive there for Brown Edge, a dispatch rider delivers the message.

Health: We have three district nurses; Nurse Ratcliffe, Nurse Clarke and Nurse Mountford. Until about two years ago we did not have a doctor living in Brown Edge, but now Dr Garrett lives at 17, Leonard Drive. There is no regular surgery in the village. A Polish doctor, from Leek, has a surgery in a lady's front room, in High Lane, and comes two half days a week.

Sandy Lane Chapel is used every other Monday for the baby clinic. Nurse Wood attends the clinic and also comes to our school. The nearest hospital is the Haywood. Mr Turner sometimes runs a bus to the N.Staffs.Royal Infirmary, on Sunday afternoons. Adults can visit two nights a week and Saturday and Sunday afternoons at the London Road hospital.

Transport: The nearest railway station is at Endon. We have a very good bus service from Brown Edge to Burslem. The first bus leaves Brown Edge at 5.48am and the last bus from

Burslem to Brown Edge leaves at 11.20pm. The first bus to Leek is at 6.37am and the last bus back leaves Leek at 12.05am. About 52 buses leave daily from Sandy Lane and School Bank to Burslem. About 24 buses go to Leek. Mr Turner runs a service to Hanley

The two buses run by
George Mayer.

A coach belonging
to Harry Hammond.

Services: Garages owned by Mr Oakes and Mr Powell mend mangles, prams, cycles and wirelesses. They also charge batteries. Mr Hammond, Mr Weaver and Mr Bourne all have taxi services in the village. There are two coal merchants- Mr Goodwin at Bank End and Brian Beech of Willfield Lane. They get their coal from Whitfield and Sneyd collieries.

Mr Hammond and Mr Booth are the village undertakers. Mr Hammond lives in Lane Ends, and keeps three taxis. Mr Booth lives at Biddulph Moor. Most residents go to the local hairdresser to have their hair cut. Mr Moore has a barber's shop and many ladies go to Mrs Garner to have their hair cut or permed.

Some fathers still repair the family shoes, but most people take them to Mr Jones, the local cobbler. There are two builders and decorators. They are Mr HN Bourne of Willfield Lane and Frost & Co. Ltd, whose workshop is at Hill Top

Street Lighting: Until about three years ago there were no streetlights in the village. The older residents did not want them. They were put up on the wooden poles that carry the overhead wires.

St Anne's bell ringers pictured outside Church House, c1940s.
Standing: Bob Cumberlidge, Billy Bourne, Bert Pointon, Bill Hollins, Dick Turner, Sam Pointon, Alan Pointon.
Seated L-R: Jonah Jolley, George Hall, Frank Holdcroft, ?.

Eric's mother, Elsie Biddulph, as the Hospital Saturday Queen at Hill Top in 1925.
Elsie is centre with Mary Durber on the left and Francis Yarwood on the right.
Back: Alice Mayer with Francis Biddulph, ?, Emma Charlesworth, Ruby Corbishley, Ida May Holdcroft, Nora Davenport, Martha Lomas, ?.
Front L-R: Lottie Holdcroft, Dorothy Lowe, Ethel Sutton, Mary Mellor, Edith Lomas, Rachel Hodgkinson,
Edith Thompson, Dolly Lancaster, Kathleen Berrisford.
2nd row: Ada Simcock, Laura Foster, Lily Simcock, ?, Lena Sherratt, ?, Edith Lomas, Florence Lomas, ?, Meda Foster.
Seated at front L-R: Mary Hannah Sutton, Gladys Foster, George Henry Sutton, Jack Bourne, Bertha Lomas.

The lights come on just before dark and go off about 11.00pm. Before we had electric lights, the only street lamp was an oil lamp, which hung over the entrance to the churchyard.

People and Work: There are about 2000 people who live in Brown Edge. Some people work in the city, about five miles away, but a lot of men work in the collieries at Whitfield and Bellerton about three miles away. Most of the women work in Leek, in the mills. The miners and mill workers have special buses to take them to work.

Churches and Chapels: The vicar at St.Anne's is Rev WTD Attoe and he lives in the vicarage. There is a Sunday school; the older children go into the church with the vicar. The younger children go into Church House with Rosemary Proctor. The church has a choir with 24 boys and men in it. The choirmaster is Mr Jack Nixon and he is also the organist. When you first become a choirboy you wear a red gown called a cassock for three months while you are on trial. If you are accepted you wear a white cloak over your cassock, called a surplice.

The church has a peal of six bells. It is exactly 100 years since a peal of bells was hung in the belfry. Mr Hall is in charge of the bells and here are some of the bell ringers: Mr Alan Pointon, Mr Bob Cumberlidge, Fred Snape, John Fenton and Robert Bailey. They practice every Monday night. Mr Hall is the vicar's warden and Mr Nixon is the people's warden. Mr Pointon, of School Bank, shares the sexton's job with Mr Simcock, of Fiddler's Bank. Mr Pointon stokes up the fires to make the church warm. Mr Simcock digs the graves and keeps the churchyard tidy. Mrs Mayer, who lives nearby, cleans the church.

Our church has a troop of scouts with Mr Fenton as Scoutmaster and Mr Nixon to advise him. There is also a youth club for boys aged 14 - 21 years, with Mr Eric Jolley as leader. The church also has a Mother's Union and Men's Society. We have three chapels, Sandy Lane, Chapel Lane and the Free Mission at Hill Top. Rev. Creber is in charge of Sandy Lane chapel helped by Mr E Goodwin. There is a youth club with Mr A Berrisford as the leader. Every Thursday a Women's Bright Hour is held and they have a speaker. Mr H Broadhurst of Biddulph takes the service in the chapel, in Chapel Lane, but when he is not there Mrs Pointon is in charge. The Free Mission has no clergyman so one of the Charlesworth family takes their services.

Leisure: There is a youth club at the YMCA (the TAB.) There is no proper sports field so children play on the small field behind the Hollybush. Sandy Lane youth club play football on the pitch at the top of Broad Lane. There is a football club belonging to the YMCA, a member of the Leek and Moorlands league.

There are five inns: The Rose and Crown, Foaming Quart, Hollybush, Lump of Coal and Roebuck. There is also a workingmen's club where there is a whist drive every Thursday night. At the YMCA you can play table tennis, darts and billiards. There is also a dance there every Thursday

night. There used to be a film show every Thursday but this has been stopped because the children did damage while the lights were out. These evenings were tried at the workingmen's club and the band room, at the Sytch, but were stopped for the same reason.

The Working Men's Club that stood in Breach Road. It was demolished in the late 1990s and new houses built on the site.

Sometimes the chapels have whist drives. The Women's Institute meets at the infant's school once a month. Mrs Williams is in charge.

Gordon Lomas

I was born in 1936 in Brindley Ford and moved to Knypersley in 1947. My dad, Joseph Lomas, was born at Hill Top, Brown Edge, in 1906. The house, on Clewlow's Bank, has been in the family for many years and my cousin Marion still lives there. Dad's father was John Lomas, who was born in 1863 and died in 1933, and I believe he lived at the Collier's Arms at one time. Grandma Lomas, John's wife, was a Sherratt before she was married, Hannah Sherratt, and came from Cowall Moor.

Grandma and Grandad Lomas had eight children, six sons and two daughters. There was Charles, Martha, Jack, Bob, Hannah, my

Gordon on left, Francis Sutton (2nd cousin) centre, Jean Sutton (cousin) right.

Grandad John Lomas and Grandma Hannah Lomas outside their cottage at Hill Top.

dad Joe and William. There was another boy Elijah who died when he was eighteen following an accident. All the boys except William were miners. Grandfather was a miner at Chatterley Whitfield all his life.

Grandfather John was one of ten children. His father was Charles Lomas, who married Martha Biddulph from Euters Hall Farm, Biddulph. Grandad had a brother, William, who was always known as Billy Muggins. He lived in a little place like a garage, near Keith's Supermarket - it's still there. My dad used to say when you visited him, he always made you very welcome. There was pretty well nothing in the place only a stove pot and a bed. When you were going he'd always say, *'on any on yer got a stray shilling?'*

My dad, Joe, used to go to Brown Edge School. He used to talk to me about Mr Jones, the headmaster. In those days you could leave school at thirteen, and go farming for twelve months, or you could stay on until you were fourteen. My father left at thirteen and went working for Walter Critchlow, at Knowles Farm, down Holehouse Lane. He did the twelve months there and lived in. He used to say he only went home for 'shirting', which meant to change your shirt or have a change of clothes.

In 1920 Dad started work on the coalface at Chatterley Whitfield Colliery. Coalface working was a dirty, difficult and dangerous occupation, particularly in those pre-mechanization days of hand-getting. The miner's tools were a pick and a shovel, coupled with dogged determination and the ability to put up with adverse conditions without complaint. The

A group of miners. Back L-R: ?, Joe Lomas (Gordon's dad)
Seated: Bob Frost, ? Bourne, ?.

height of the seam in which Dad worked was 27 inches. He spent most of his time either kneeling on a cold wet floor or lying on his side 'picking' at the coal. Dad's other great love was his garden, and whenever he took up his spade to dig the soil, he would automatically drop to one knee. He couldn't work standing up!

Dad was a good pianist and spent his evenings entertaining his family with his favourite tunes and hymns. However, after an accident at work which damaged his right hand, he still played, but with difficulty. He was a total teetotaller and so was his family. They were strong Methodists and attended Hill Top Chapel at Brown Edge. I've still got some of Dad's prizes.

Dad gave in all some 44 years service to Chatterley Whitfield and sadly after enjoying only three years of retirement in his beloved garden, he had another heart attack and that was it. He died in 1967 at the age of 60. Most of his fellow workers who worked on the low seams, in those bad conditions, died around the age of 60. They all lie there together in Biddulph Churchyard.

Joseph Lomas (Gordon's dad) 1955.

Joseph Lomas on the right, with his brother Charlie 1950.

When Chatterley Whitfield Mining Museum opened, the director of the museum contacted me. He knew of me from the guides who worked at the museum and knew that I had some of my father's items that he used in his work. He wanted to spotlight my father as an example of a working miner, and display the items in a glass case. I'd got Dad's clogs, his lamp, his respirator, his pick and belts. The miners wore very thick heavy duty belts because they had to carry so much on them - battery for their hand lamp, pick, snappin tin, respirator etc.

It was impossible to take a watch down the pit as it would get broken, but they needed to know when to come up off the shift. Dad had a timepiece, in a brass case, in the shape of a pocket watch. It had to be brass because it was one of the few materials that are allowed underground, because of sparking. All the items I loaned to the museum were officially handed over. I still have the press release for the opening of 'The Collier's Story.'

Many people used to wear clogs. Farmers wore them and the women who worked in the fustian mills preferred them. The miner's clogs were a little different. All villages in the coalfield area had a clogger - a man who had the measurements of your feet. He would make a wooden mould of your feet and keep that for whenever you went for new clogs. In good clogs the wooden sole was made out of alder wood from the forests in Germany. Alder wood does not shrink and it does not crack in wet conditions. The miners were sometimes working in water. The upper part of the clog was leather and was attached to the wooden sole with welting, which was either leather or copper. The uppers lasted for many years but the heel and sole, even with tips on, only lasted about six months. So you went to the clogger who had your measurements, and he'd attach a new sole with another piece of welting.

I always remember when Dad went back to work after his accident, he said *'We've got to get all the coal out of Chatterley Whitfield.'* I thought that sounds good, it sounds as if they'll be getting coal for evermore. Little did we realise it would soon close, with all the other mines in the Stoke-on-Trent area - what a waste!

My mother was Sarah Jane Haydon and she was born at Sand's Cottage, Marshes Hill. Harvey Durber lived there at one time. The family moved to Ladymoor gate on the Lask Edge road, and then they moved to Childerplay Farm, Bemersley Road, now demolished. Mother's parents were Thomas William and Alice Maud Haydon. Grandfather worked at Robert Heath's Iron Works but also on the farm. He didn't own the farm but rented it from the Heath's Estate. They then moved to a shop in Brindley Ford, No 7 High Street where they sold sweets and crocks. I was born at the shop and the property is still standing today.

The Haydon family originated from Devonshire. Two brothers came working as navies on the railway, married two local girls and settled here. My Great Grandfather, Thomas William, was born in 1844 and married Sarah Jane Hickman. They had 18 children over 25 years. Two of the children died young. They celebrated their diamond wedding on October 8th 1927 with a family gathering. I have a newspaper cutting of the occasion.

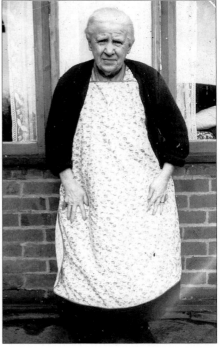

Gordon's grandma, Alice Maud Haydon 1950.

Wedding of Hannah Lomas (Dad's sister) and Jesse Sutton 1916. Back, right Charlie Lomas. Front centre Bob Lomas (Dad's brother)
Seated: Grandma Hannah Lomas, ?, Martha Lomas, Jesse and Hannah, ?, John Lomas and Grandad John Lomas.

Back: Sam Pointon, Joe Haydon, Joe Lomas. Seated: Edith Stonier, Jane Jervis, Sarah Haydon.

Robert Lomas (Dad's brother) with family, c1932.
L-R: Nellie, Edith, Robert, Vera and Doris.

CHATTERLEY WHITFIELD PRESS INFORMATION.

On Friday, March 27th, 1992 at 1.00pm, Mr Gordon Lomas will be visiting Chatterley Whitfield Mining Museum with his wife to open a Lamp house exhibition which celebrates the Whitfield Colliery career of his father Joe.

Joseph Lomas was born at Hill Top, Brown Edge on May 12th, 1906, the second son from a family of eight, which comprised six sons involved at the mine for much of their working lives.

With the exception of a brief involvement at Bellerton Colliery between 1921 and 1924 Joe worked continually at Chatterley Whitfield until his death in 1967. From 1924 to 1944 Joe was a face worker or collier, cutting coal in the Middle Pit. Unfortunately in June 1944 Joe suffered a serious accident when a fall of coal severed a nerve in his right hand reducing control of his fingers. For five years Joe served as a pump operator but his desire was always to return to the coal face, and this he achieved in 1949. Joe continued at the face until his death in 1967. In a colliery which enjoyed a high reputation for the commitment and hard work of its colliers. Joe Lomas established a deserved reputation for loyalty, often returning to the pit or stopping on after his daily shift had ended, if there were problems to be solved or mates underground to be helped.

Joe Lomas' involvement at Chatterley Whitfield coincided with the hey-day of the site which first commenced operations in the late 1850s. During Joe's Whitfield career (1924-67) mine mechanisation and innovative engineering practice saw Chatterley Whitfield Britain's first million ton per annum colliery with employment for over 3,000 local men in all colliery occupations.

The eldest child of Thomas William and Sarah Jane had a tragic accident in 1886. John was employed as a forge boy at Robert Heath's ironworks and like others from the area, spent his leisure time around the Knypersley Pool countryside. During the winter of 1886 the severe night frosts created thick sections of ice on the Serpentine Lake, where John and his pals enjoyed skating. They became familiar with the area of the pool that was of a good thickness. On Friday 13th March, before work,

Childerplay Farm c1916. Grandma Alice Maud Haydon centre with daughter Elizabeth & son Joe. The NCB started tipping coal waste in the area during the 1960s. The farmhouse was left to the last, demolished and buried c1969. The Hill family were the last to live there.

John went for his usual skate on the ice-covered section. Unfortunately a flock of ducks and water hens had been in the water, just before midnight, and this prevented certain parts from freezing. When John skated on the section where the fowl had been, he disappeared into the extreme depths of the water and drowned. He was eighteen years of age.

Grandfather Haydon, when he rented Childerplay Farm off Mr William Heath, used to poach on the Greenway Bank Estate. Grandad was a keen poacher and a good shot and was often warned by Mr Heath to keep away from the grounds around the Hall. Mr Heath became tired of sending these warnings, and early one summer morning Grandad was spotted in the grounds collecting the odd rabbit for the evening meal. Mr Heath decided to handle the situation himself

Gordon's great grand parents Thomas William and Sarah Haydon with their family 1892.
Back row: Sarah Jane, Annie, Andrew, Harry, Thomas William, Jim, Sam Oakes (son-in-law)
Seated: Lizzie, Great Grandad, Great Grandma, Alice Maud (Grandma), Emma.
Front: children George, Ted, Sam , Myna and John Haydon (Jack)

and went with his gun in search of the poacher. He heard a rustling in some of the rhododendron bushes and paraded around the outside, while Grandad traversed round the inside. Eventually Mr Heath gave up the chase and sent a message that if he had spotted Grandad he would have fired without any hesitation. Grandad returned a message saying he would have done likewise - and he reminded Mr Heath that he had a double-barrelled gun and would have fired both barrels. Grandfather poached for many more rabbits, and they both lived to a ripe old age.

Jack Haydon.

My mother's brother, John Haydon, known as Jack, was a well-known character in the area. He lived at Brown Edge, but then moved to Biddulph and later formed the business of Haydon and Sons, transporting livestock. He died in 1991, at the age of 99.

I have always been interested in local and mining history and also local dialect. These are some of the mining terms that were used in local mines - I feel these need to be recorded.

GENERAL TERMS
Bank - head of pit shaft
Banksman - top of pit
Setter on - bottom of pit
Loose it - end of shift
Hammed, sawnit and buzzed - late for work
Lumpy tums - porridge made of oatmeal

Road cod - putting rails in; keep coal flowing
Man hole - recess in crut or main roadway
Delfman - pit worker
Delf Hole - pit shaft
Delf Rags - miner's clothing
Daytaler - odd job man in pit

UNDERGROUND TERMS
Werrent - floor in pit
Gob - area where coal has been extracted
Fire damp - compound of hydrogen and phosphorous causes explosion when ignited
Methane gas - fire damp
Black damp - mixture of carbon dioxide and nitrogen which will suffocate.
Thurl - to drill or pierce a hole
Wapps - points which switch tracks on lines
Jim crow - bar for switching tracks
Banjo - metal water bottle
Crut - off main roadway
Gobb leggeder - three pronged fork
Snapping - food taken by miners

Chatterley Whitfield Colliery.

Robert John Bailey

I was born in 1944 on this farm, Greenway Bank. My father was John Bailey and my mother was Edith Holdcroft. My maternal grandparents were John and Charlotte Holdcroft from Judgfields Farm. Mother had three sisters, Hilda, Alice and Elizabeth. I never knew Alice or Elizabeth. Auntie Hilda was married to Arthur Simcock and they farmed at Springbank Farm, Clay Lake, Endon. All four sisters went to Brown Edge School.

My paternal grandparents were John and Rosanna Bailey who started their farming career at Brandy Lee Farm in Rushton. I think they moved to Knypersley End Farm, Knypersley, as tenants to the Heaths around 1906. It was somewhere in the region of 1911 when they actually came to farm here, at Greenway Bank.

Grandmother's sister Jane, and her husband, Tom Finney, were tenants here before them. Tom died in 1907 at the age of 46. Jane was then left with three children, and a large farm to manage, so that's how my grandfather came to be here. Jane left and he got the tenancy of Greenway Bank Farm, another Heath farm under the same estate, but a larger one of about 140 acres. A portion of the Biddulph Estate, 1686 acres and 22 dairy farms and other lots, owned by Robert Heath, was put up for sale in 1919. It was then that Grandfather bought Greenway Bank Farm. We now farm in excess of 220 acres, having bought adjoining land.

When I was born, Grandfather lived here, and Uncle James, who never married, besides my parents. I have three sisters, all older - Margaret, Elizabeth and Hilda. I was the youngest - a son at last. I'm told that Grandfather 'celebrated' that night!

We always kept poultry and pigs - about five breeding sows.   My early memories are that pigs were grown a lot bigger then than they are today. Quite often we'd have one killed for ourselves by Mr Proctor from Biddulph Moor. You had to get a licence to kill a pig in those days. You never had pork or pigs killed in a month that hadn't got an 'r' in it - because there were no 'fridges' then. Plenty of hot water was required to scrape off the hairs and then the pig was hung. The head was made into brawn, and the blood was used for black pudding. Big blocks of salt were used to cure the bacon. The sides of pig

Robert with his sisters 1949: Elizabeth, Margaret, Robert & Hilda.

were laid out on stone stillages in the pantry and we had to keep rubbing the salt into the flesh over numerous days. I remember helping - it was a cold job! The jointed hams would then be covered with muslin to keep the flies off and hung from a beam. It'd keep till you'd eaten it!

We had a milk round until about 1962. We delivered to Bemersley and New Buildings, Mill Hayes Road, Park Lane Estate, Knypersley, Blue Gates Bank, and then back to Brindley Ford. We helped on the round as soon as we were big enough - as soon as we could carry milk

Robert's mum, Edith Holdcroft 1930.

Grandma Charlotte Holdcroft at Judgefield Farm c1939.

John Bailey Snr. in his WW I uniform.

RIGHT:
Grandad John Holdcroft at Judgefield Farm, c1940.

Robert's dad John Bailey and his grandad John Bailey Snr. delivering milk in Brindley Ford c1914.

bottles we went with Dad. I didn't do it very often - my sisters would probably say I hardly ever did! The round was done seven days a week, even on Christmas Day. We never missed. Originally, Dad and Grandfather delivered the milk in churns using measures - a quart, a pint, and a half pint - to ladle it into customer's jugs when they came out of their homes to collect it. Grandfather used to say that he was asked not to ring his bell on Sunday mornings because people in the churches (there were three in Brindley Ford) came out if they heard Johnny Bailey's bell. They wouldn't want to miss the milkman!

John Bailey Snr. and his milk van, c1960.

We were asked to do all sorts of errands on the milk round. People used to give you their accumulators to be taken to Percy Lloyd's Redcross Garage to be charged up. Then you'd always got customers who would have relatives on the round and they'd ask you to take notes for them. You became involved with families. I can remember christenings on Sunday morning and being offered sherry, even at a young age. It was the same when somebody died. I can remember going in with my dad to see some old lady who was laid out in the parlour - because you'd think nothing of it in those days.

We had a big patch of rhubarb in the garden and before we went with the milk we'd be sent to pick some, bundle it up and sell it on the round. Also, Mrs Hepplethwaite at Mill Hayes House had a large greenhouse and the same applied when there were loads of tomatoes. If the Hepplethwaites were away and there was no gardener about, we used to have to go in the greenhouse and pick some tomatoes, weigh'em and bag them up in brown bags - there's nothing that smells nicer! We also used to take Mr Heath's washing down to Nellie Whalley in Brindley Ford on Mondays. It'd come back on Thursday, all ironed and smelling nice. By this time the Heath's own laundry was a laundry no more - it had been sold.

Grandfather Bailey was quite strict. He didn't need to say much - you got the gist with just the look - because I was quite naughty. I burnt the hayshed down when I was four. The hay sheds on the estate were quite unique. They had hollow cast iron pillars, timber trusses and a tile roof. There was always a box of matches on the oil stove in the kitchen, and one day I was with a friend and as I went out, I just happened to pick the box up. It seemed great fun striking those matches on the cast iron pillars - next thing, it was blazing from one end to the other and we ran like the clappers! The following day I remember sitting under the table and all those black boots of the firemen and police inquiring as to how it had happened. Fred Chaddock always said that it was the best crop of wheat they'd ever harvested!

I went to Brindley Ford Primary School and we had to walk there. I passed my 11+ and went to Wolstanton Grammar School. My homework often got left until the last, farm work came first; well, you do what you enjoy doing most. I think anyone brought up on a farm enjoys what's going on. I don't remember having pocket money, not as such. When there was work to be done you just got on with it. We never wanted for anything - we never went short of anything. I suppose it was the early form of work experience. If we were missing for long, there was always an 'enquiry' when we got back - absent without leave.

To get to Wolstanton School I travelled on a Stanier's bus and caught it at the Railway Hotel, which was later to become the Matador. There were three busloads of boys from Biddulph then.

One of my very few holidays was when we went to Penmaenmawr in Wales for a week at the age of about four. There was Mother, us 4 children, my cousin Alan Simcock, and Auntie Cissie, (Ann, my father's sister). Dick Gilchrist took us in the milk van. It only had a driver's seat so we sat on upturned milk crates, wooden egg boxes or stools with cushions on. (Seat belts not an option then) As food was still on ration, we took our own provisions for the week. Whilst there we visited what was once the Heath Convalescent Home at Llanfairfechan.

In 1954 I went to visit Bamfords at Uttoxeter, invited by John West & Sons of Derby Street, Leek, farm machinery dealers at that time - and we bought our first pickup baler. That factory, to a ten year old, was out of this world, We actually watched the construction of machinery, the welders, and the paint shop, draftsmen - you name it. In the factory there were rows and rows of stationary engines, all waiting for export, all painted green. In another part were 7RTC-mowing machines based on the original horse-drawn design but then enlarged and improved, to be drawn by tractors, incorporating the new self-lift cutter bar.

We had two full-time workers on the farm. Fred Chaddock, who initially cycled from Harriseahead, and the other was Jess Corbishley from New Buildings. Then you'd also have elderly gentlemen, shall I put it that way, who did seasonal or maintenance work. There was Tom Cumberlidge from Bemersley, who did hedge laying and green crop thinning, and Jack Wild from New Buildings. We grew potatoes, mangolds or swedes, winter wheat, oats and ox cabbage to feed to the cattle. We used to put in about 12,000 cabbage plants.

1954 was quite an important year because legislation was introduced that anyone who retailed milk had to have cattle that were TB free. Following veterinary advice it was decided to replace all our cattle, so the entire herd was sold at Leek Market. We then replaced our herd with heifers bought in from designated areas that had been TB free for some while. We started off with about nine and slowly built it up. We kept adding stock from Wales. The Welsh farmers were changing from dairy shorthorns, the traditional British breed, and were using black and white Friesian bulls. As a result the progeny sometimes came blue-coloured. These were very good cattle and they were known in the trade as first crosses. 1954 was a very wet summer too, and that was the last time I heard a corncrake. I remember it called all summer, across by Dallows Wood and I've never heard one since!

After harvesting our wheat and oats, the threshing machine would come later in the year. Now that was something that sticks in your mind as a child! The threshing box that came used to belong to John Sidebottom and Sons. I've often thought about all the pulley wheels - there were no guards on anything. There were flat belts flying round and it was very seldom that anyone got hurt. The 'little lad's' job was to bag the chaff and you always got your eyes full of dust. It was fed to the cows in the spring to bulk the feed up. The threshed straw went through a stationary baler which used wire as ties. You always had some mice and rats in the stack, so we used to run chicken netting all round the bottom about a yard away. When the rats ran out you had chance to clobber them.

Coming back to cattle, there are a lot of people who originated in this area who have become well known pedigree breeders, one being Clive Pickford from Lower Stonehouse. He moved to Spot Grange, Hilderstone. His grandchildren are running the farm now, and recently they've bred a bull called Picston Shottle, which is one of the top ranking bulls in the world.

I married Margaret Holdcroft in 1969; she used to live at Knypersley Mill Farm. In 1958 Margaret and her family left Knypersley Mill and moved into Gardeners House. We have three children, Mark, Richard and Joanne, and two granddaughters, Rosanna and Olivia.

My two sons are milking about130 mainly pedigree Holstein cows now. As we rear all our own replacements the total number of the herd is around 230 head. We've had milking machines as long as I can remember but Dad taught me to milk by hand, in case of a power failure. Today, we have our own stand-by generator. We have bigger milk storage tanks now and the milk is collected on alternate days.

I have seen lots of changes in farming in my lifetime and lots more rules and regulations. Although the principles remain the same, living on a dairy farm is no longer the way of life it once was. Since the introduction of milk quotas in 1984, the BSE scare in 1996, the foot and mouth outbreaks in February 2001 and 2007, plus the current ongoing TB crisis it has become an ever-rising mountain of paperwork, licences, disinfection routines and regular inspections. Our family have farmed at Greenway Bank for nearly 100years - our two sons being the fourth generation.

Uncle James with the family.
L-R: Harold Abbott, Uncle
James, Nora Abbott, Joanne
Bailey, Robert Holdcroft holding
Richard and Mark Bailey.

BELOW:
Hedgelaying at Bailey's farm
c1940. L-R: 2nd Joseph
Haydon, 6th Jacker Berrisford,
7th John Bailey Snr.

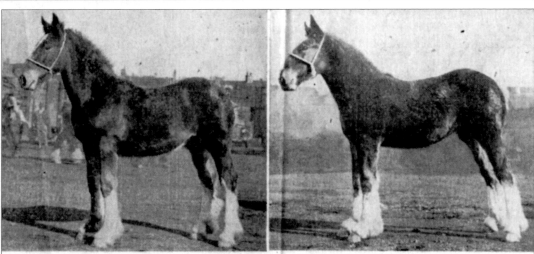

Champion and reserve champion at Newcastle and District Shire Horse Society's annual foal show held at Newcastle Smithfield—the colt exhibited by Mr. John Bailey, of Greenway Bank, Brindley Ford, and the filly sent by Mr. A. M. Holdcroft, of College Fields, Woore. The colt won the Twyford Cup.

Ethel Dawson née Sutton

I was born in this house on Clewlows Bank, Hill Top, in 1918. My parents were Arthur and Elizabeth Georgina Sutton. Mother's maiden name was Knight. There were 6 of us children, 3 boys and 3 girls, Mabel, Bill, Arthur, Gladys, George Henry and me. Gladys died of pneumonia when she was eight years and nine months. Father worked at Chatterley Whitfield colliery and walked there every day.

Ethel's sister, Gladys.

Mother was left this cottage by an uncle who lived here before us. I think his name was Smith. It used to be a one up and one down cottage. Tomkinsons used to live in the old cottage in front of us. Honor Dawson, when she was young, used to live where Wardles live now. Frank Holdcroft, who was half-brother to Miss Dawson, used to live in the first house in Back Lane, opposite Marshes Hill. I remember when I was a young woman, there was a real bad lightening storm, it hit Holdcroft's house and did quite a bit of damage. The chimney was blown off and the meter was blown out. The family were in the house at the time, unharmed but very shocked.

Where Boltons live, they call that Brick Bank up there. There used to be a brickyard in the field opposite but it was before my time. We used to have to fetch all the water from Star Well. We carried it in zinc buckets, which were heavy before you started. When there was no water at Star Well we used to go down Grizzer Hole, down the fields where Iris Mayer used to live. We used to go right down there to the wood, and coming back, halfway up we often used to fall and drop the buckets and have to go back again. On Monday mornings, washday, we used to have to fetch it from the well, fill the boiler ready for washing and fill a spare tub for rinsing.

I always went to Charlesworth's Mission at Hill Top - it was a really nice little place. They don't go to Sunday school now - chapels and churches closing, it doesn't sound right. When I was in Canada there was a new church there and there were cars for miles and miles - it was packed. The mission was run by Ralph Charlesworth and then later by Ralph's sons, Eber, Jack and Wilf. Sometimes we used to go in the field near the mission and have a tea party and a treat. They were good times.

I loved school. Mrs Jones, the headmaster's wife, was very nice. She was a lady she was. She wanted someone to help in the greenhouse and I was

Ethel with her brothers Bill and George Henry (right).

Ethel's mother, Elizabeth Georgina Sutton, (née Knight) with two of her children, Mabel on left and Bill on right.

Mother and Dad, Arthur and Elizabeth G Sutton, in the 1940s.

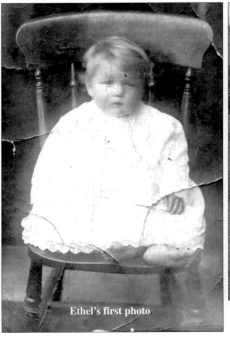

Ethel's first photo

Daughter June with friends at Hill Top in the early 1950s.
L-R: Heather Cotterill, Shirley Brassington, June Dawson and Linda Harvey.

chosen to go because I'd passed my exams. We did so much, then we went into the headmaster's house and she made me coffee

We really liked working in the gardens. The teachers were Miss Davenport, Miss Stonier and Miss Dawson. There was a Mr Downing but he left and Mr Evans came. Mr Jones, the headmaster, was very strict but I think that's what they need today - it was great.

I left at 14 and went working at Stannards, up Buxton Road. Well you started off doing errands, and then you started on the button making, a farthing a dozen. They were fabric-covered buttons and there were dozens of them on blouses in those days. They made all the dresses for Marks and Spencers. They were sold for five bob each but we used to get 'em at half a crown. We worked on piecework and worked like the devil.

They used to run no end of buses from everywhere into Leek for the mill girls. I liked it in the mill but one day my sister, Mabel, came to visit and my life changed. Mabel was married and living at Barlaston. She told my mother that that they wanted someone at the boss's farm, to live in. My mother said *'Ooh our Bet can go there.'* So off I went.

I lived in at the farm and you'd never finished there. Billy and Mary Johnson kept it and it was near Meaford power station. I used to have to help with the haymaking, getting potatoes and all sorts of things. I was about 17 when I went and stayed until I was in my early twenties. It was a dairy farm but they had pigs, about 200 turkeys and they planted turnips, mangolds and potatoes.

They had a milking machine. I used to have to carry the milk in and I used to have to scrub all the pans out in cold water. We had breakfast then I had to scrub the pans in boiling soda water. There was a massive furnace and they used to go in there to be boiled. While the pans were in there I had to scrub the milk house out.

It was like being at home and you had all your meals with the family. When I first went there I couldn't eat the big breakfasts but they told me I'd got to. They said everybody had to have two eggs there. When it was threshing time all the men who were working there used to come in for their dinner. We used to have to peel a hundredweight of potatoes the night before. There was a massive joint of beef. When they were all fed we had our dinner and then did the washing up - I thought we were never going to finish that washing up!

They were great people though. They had two young children, Arthur and Kathleen, and everywhere I went they followed me. At nights we used to go a walk through the big wood, with a bag of toffees, and there used to be loads and loads of pheasants. I remember there was a lamb that we used to feed with a bottle and it used to follow me and the children just like a dog. Once when I was going home it followed me to the bus and I had to take it back. I missed the bus then had to go the long way home on the train. I used to go home every other weekend.

They had a round for potatoes and when they were busy I helped them out. Everybody was after the potatoes 'cos they were straight from the farm. The lady used to drive the van

Ethel at the farm with Kathleen (the farmer's daughter) and the friendly lamb.

and I used to take the potatoes to the doors, in half hundredweight sacks. I got more money taking potatoes than I did wages.

I left the farm in my early twenties and, as the war was on, I went to work at Swynnerton, the ordnance factory. I worked on tracer bullets there. The shell used to go with the cordite in then we used to put the bullet on the top, with the powder in. We used to just keep putting them through the machine. You didn't have to watch it as you knew what you were doing.

I remember there was a girl from Burslem called May Joynson and she was the most beautiful singer I've ever heard. She'd be singing at the top of her voice and we all used to join in with her. All of a sudden there'd be these loud pinging noises - they were faulty tracer bullets going off and hitting the ceiling. There were all different sorts of ammunition done in different blocks on the site.

When we worked shifts, every so often we had to go down, in twos, to see the outside range to see them trying the bullets out. It was an education and so noisy! After I'd been there a few years Hilda Jones, who was in the office, wanted somebody to help her and she thought I seemed pretty good. I thought, *'What the devil have I done?'* I'd never done any office work but I ended up in the office with her. I really enjoyed it though and it was all days.

In some of the blocks there was danger. You went over the bridge to one block where they worked on yellow powder. I had to fetch their clocking on cards and my hands, just picking the cards out, were as yellow as anything. A man from Norton Green who used to work in it was really yellow - he looked awful. We couldn't get hurt where we were because there were cages round and you just had to put your hands through. Loads of people worked at Swynnerton. It was very interesting.

My husband, Rob, was born at Hill Top as well and I have always known him. We have been married nearly 60 years and I think we are the oldest married couple up here. I have always known my friend Elsie Rowland as well and she still lives at Hill Top. Elsie's auntie used to keep a shop up here and George Mayer kept his bus there. There used to be a shop in Jack Berrisford's yard and my mum used to tell me there was one opposite the Rose and Crown, where Lunts live. Fred Sheldon (Numpy) mended shoes at East View. It used to be half a crown to have them soled and heeled then. I wonder what it costs now? - I suppose people just throw them away now and buy new - no make do and mend these days.

I remember, along Back Lane, all the old men used to gather there and play shotties - I've still got a box of them now. When our children were young my friend, Nancy Harvey, and I used to hold ends of a skipping rope across the road so the children could all skip in. It used to be so quiet.

I still love living at Hill Top although we have no buses up here now. Fortunately I can still get about and am pretty active. We have lovely views here and the air is good.

Ethel with her husband, Rob.

Frank Lynch - Lower Stonehouse Farm

I first came up to Brown Edge in 1937 to help out old Mr Pickford, who farmed at Lower Stonehouse. I was an only child and when my father died when I was only nine, mother and I went back to live with Grandma in Albion Street, Middleport. Mr Pickford used to deliver milk round Middleport and our house was his toilet stop. Bob Cumberlidge worked for him too and he was sweet on our May, who was my Auntie and lived with us.

It was August holidays and I was standing at the bottom of the entry this particular day, Mr Pickford was on his own and he said *'What're you doing Frankie?'* I said *'Nothing Mr Pickford.'* So he goes and says to my grandmother *'Can Frankie come and help me out delivering milk'.* As I knew a lot of the streets and a lot of the people this is what I did.

Mr Pickford delivered the milk in a Ford V8 van. There were about four or five churns of milk and small cans. The customers had jugs and we poured the milk into those. They used to leave the jugs outside with a saucer on top. We collected the money at the weekend. I remember once, I was in Maddock Street and had collected half a

Frank, aged 10, looking a bit glum because it was meat and potato pie night and he was reluctant to leave it.

crown, given the change and was flicking the coin as I went along. Well I missed it and it went straight down a grid. Honest I daresn't tell him. I made an excuse to go home, and when I told my mother she gave me the half crown - oh dear!

Anyway, one particular weekend, Mr Pickford invited me to come over to his farm. Well, me a townie, coming out into the country, I thought it was great. I went as often as I could after that and Mrs Pickford took to me. I went over at weekends and holidays. The priest at Church wanted to know where I was. I stayed at the farm as much as I could, when I was needed. At haymaking time I'd live there and have my own room. They had an only son, Clive, who was in his late twenties.

They had two big hen sheds down the fields with about 150 to 200 hens. I used to collect the eggs for Mrs Pickford. They also had about 15 to 20 pigs and kept them in two houses. I used to sit wiping the piglets when they'd been born, putting them in a safe place, so the sow didn't roll on them. I enjoyed it all - I was never ever bored. Mrs Pickford used to call me Mr Pickford's shadow, because I was always behind him like. I think the farm was about 90 acres.

I worked on the farm from 1937 to 1941. Mr Pickford's name was William. He was a strict man but fair. He was a very serious type of man. Mrs Pickford was a schoolteacher. They had about 90 cows and we were always up at five o'clock in a morning. There were three or four men milking and every cow was milked by hand. Bob Cumberlidge helped and Mr Pickford's son, Clive. My job was taking the milk down the dairy, and putting it through the cooler, into the churn. Mrs Pickford was also in the dairy. It took about two hours to milk and clean up. After a big breakfast in the kitchen, we liked to set off delivering by nine o'clock. We were delivering until about three or four o'clock. There was no time to get bored. We milked again

Lower Stonehouse Farm.

about six o'clock and it was about 7.30 to 8.00 pm when we finished.

Mrs Pickford was a wonderful cook and we always had a big dinner with pudding, sometimes junket, which is like a blancmange. We'd have a nice big blob of cream on. I was never hungry. It was a big kitchen with a beautiful olde world fireplace with an open fire. We had all our meals there. There were two ways to go upstairs, one on either side of the fireplace. My bedroom just had a bed and sideboard and it had a lovely view but it also overlooked the outside toilet. I don't remember any electricity - it was always oil lamps. There were three or four around the room, with a big one on the table. They gave a lovely glow. We used a storm lamp when we went out milking.

I remember there was a big cold room down the passage with big sides of bacon hanging up and jugged hare - ooh it was cold.

When I left school I got a job at the Co-op. I wanted to be a car mechanic, but at the Co-op, before you did anything else, you had to do eighteen months to two years on the bread vans. When I was supposed to start on the Monday, Mr Bond, the manager at the yard, said I was being loaned out to Mr Pickford. I think Mr Bond and Mr Pickford were friends, and I was loaned out for two weeks, because Mr Pickford had got no help.

After we had delivered the milk, every other Tuesday, we used to call at Parker's Brewery in Burslem. When they'd been brewing at the weekend, they used to bag up all the spent hops. Mr Pickford used to buy some bags and load the van up. The hops were mixed with feed and the cattle loved it. I remember one time coming down Norton Green with Bob Cumberlidge driving, and me in the back with the hops. The van started to sway because it was overloaded at the back, and the front wheels were off the road. I was swaying around in the back drunk with the fumes.

I used to love haymaking time. My job was holding the horse and driving it on to the next batch when they'd loaded the hay. We always cut six foot all round the field with the scythe first, to get the machine in. Bert Pointon always came down to help and there was a chap called Paul from Old Lane. There was also a very nice young fellow from Heath's Row. I think his name was Tommy Holdcroft. He was a bit older than me but we were close friends. He was very good looking and smart, but I have not been able to find out what happened to him. I may have the name wrong.

I used to help forking the hay over. Once we got it up to the farm my job was treading it down as the men were chucking it into the barn. When we'd finished everyone would sit down to a big meal in the kitchen. I helped Mrs Pickford carry the meals in and then we would clear everything off before we had our meal. Haymaking time was the only time Mr Pickford had any alcohol on the farm. When I was older I went home on the bus after haymaking. I used to catch Turner's bus at five to ten and my parents paid my bus fare. All the time I was at the farm I never remember receiving any money off Mr Pickford, just bed and board.

At night time there was always something to do. A job I loved doing was identifying the cattle that had been born. I had a big sheet of paper and prints of cattle markings. I had to try and give a registered description of the calves - that's how they registered in those days. The table would be covered with all these papers and Mrs Pickford would say, *'Come on Frankie - your bedtime.'* The forms would be sent off to the Ministry.

Mr Pickford always kept a bull. I think he was the only farmer locally who had one. I remember it pinned him up a corner once and someone had to rescue him with a pitchfork. A couple of times I was asked to walk the bull up to the next farm - its services were required! I think the farmer was named Jarvis and it's where Barrie Scott lives now. I walked the bull up using a 5-foot wooden pole. It had like a ring clip at the end, which was fastened to the bull's nose. I had to fetch the bull back after 2 or 3 hours, not knowing anything about what he'd been up to!

We always used to have a wash at the kitchen sink because there was no bathroom. We used to wipe our hands on a sugar bag first to get most of the wet off, and then finish off with a towel. They were big hessian bags, about six foot square, with Tate and Lyle stamped on. They were used as carpet in the hall, or cut down and used for towels.

Frank with his wife Marjorie in their garden at Brown Edge.

I always remember the old bench toilet which was outside. It had two holes in it, one for adults and a smaller one alongside for young children. I goes to the toilet one day, and as there was nobody about I thought I would sit on the grown-up side. I'm sitting there nice and comfortable, and Mr Pickford came in (They called him 'Boss'). He just looked at me and said *'Move over there, that's yours'.* I moved over and we both sat there together - it's true that is. When it needed emptying, if I was there it was my job - I was the chosen one. I had to shovel it into a barrow and then it was buried in a hole down the bottom of the field. The sights and smell of the countryside were something that you accepted. There was always an animal muck ruck at the back of the farm.

My wife Marjorie and I came to live at Brown Edge in 1985. We had lived in a big house in Leek Road but when our three sons left, we wanted somewhere smaller. When we all sat down to discuss it I said, *'There's only one place I want to go - Brown Edge'* and that's what we did. When we moved in I was looking forward to seeing Bob Cumberlidge again, but sadly he'd died a month beforehand. It is great to be living at Brown Edge where I had such happy times as a child. When Mr Pickford died Clive and his mother moved to Spotacre, Hilderstone, and we went to visit them once. John Lovatt, who now lives a Lower Stonehouse showed me round the farm once and that stirred lots of memories for me. I had a great time.

Roy Snape - Brown Edge Football Club

Many village football teams have proudly played their part in the history of Staffordshire Moorland's football. The village of Brown Edge has every reason to feel especially proud of their team's achievements.

The Brown Edge love of football started before the First World War. When I was talking to some of the old people on the village they told me there used to be five teams. This was probably by 1930. In the fifties the village team became known as Brown Edge FC and they later chose the rustic colours of amber and black, for their club colours.

One of the first achievements of the village team is little known. In the 50s Brown Edge travelled to the city ground to play Stoke City Reserves in the semi-final of the Staffordshire Cup. In front of a large crowd the village lads pulled off a remarkable 2-0 win and finished runners-up in the final.

The 1960s found the Edge playing in the Burslem & Tunstall League, where they picked up League and Cup honours. The team's results always used to be put up in the window of Mr Moore's barber's shop - it's where Sid's hairdressers is now. I always remember when we were kids, my brother Barry and I used to rush home from Endon School to the shop to see the results and team selection. How excited we were, never thinking that we would both be playing for the team one day. As young lads we were very proud of our Edge!

In the 70s the team was managed by the highly respected Tommy Jones and the 'Edge' moved to the Leek and Moorland League, in Division II. They were a great team and promotion quickly followed to Division I. They did not have to wait long before this talented team achieved the Division I championship. They completed the double by winning the League Cup with a stunning goal from Barry Snape in extra time. Unfortunately the team could not make it a treble, losing to rival village team Ipstones in the final of the Leek Post Charity Shield.

The following season the team were runners up in Division I but again reached the final of the League Cup. They played at Leek Town against Ipstones, but this time the Edge eased to a 4-1 victory. A few days later the team stepped out once again to play in the final of the Leek Post Charity Shield. A 5-1 thrashing of Leek United saw the Edge lift the trophy for the first time in their history.

The team used to play at one time in the field behind where Mosedales lived, at Hobbs House. Then they played up at Broad Lane, and later in a field behind Fairfield Avenue.

I remember once there was a girl down Norton Green with cancer and they were raising money to send her to a specialist in America. A charity match was organised between the Edge and a professional team who had all played for the Vale at one time. I think Colin Leek and Jock McLean had got it together. We played on a pitch behind the old school at Norton Green and got changed in the Foaming Quart. It was absolutely packed; there were so many people round the field. We were a good team and were pretty fit. We loved our football and it just happened that we managed to get all the right players together at the right time. As my brother and I were walking towards the pitch, this bloke on the professional team turned to this other one and said *'Let's keep it down to nine cos it is for charity!'* Well me and my brother were fuming. We were never in awe of professionals because we knew some of them. Well it was a draw 4 all, as our last two goals were disallowed.

Jock McLean was a fabulous footballer. He used to play in Scotland, and then when he moved to the village I think he played for Cellarhead first. He played for Brown Edge when he was 29 or 30 and he played for the Vale. He knew all the Vale boys. He'd got something that he passed on to us. We had this respect for him. He had a fantastic shot - he could knock you out. I remember once we were playing Leigh United and the goalkeeper hated Jock. We had a penalty; Jock took it and struck the ball so hard that you saw the pegs fly out at the back. It went straight under the net. The goalie started laughing and said to Jock *'I knew you'd miss.'* The ref said, *'Miss! He hit it that hard he took the pegs out'*

We had a lot of good footballers on the village but they didn't all play for the village team. Frankie Sromek became semi-professional. Mark, Kevin and Peter Sromek were also very good players. Chris and Eddy Wood were two others, and Robert Mountford played for the Vale. Robert's brother Ian played a bit for the village team. Leslie Wood was the fastest sprinter at that time. My brother Barry was a fantastic left-winger - he used to get fifty odd goals in a season. All five Snape brothers played for the village. As well as Barry and me there was Tony, Terry and Keith. We all won something with the Edge. In the 70s, without a doubt, the backbone of the team was David Condliffe.

Although the Edge continued to add to their honours list, the village lads' last achievement was their finest. They beat Staffordshire County Premier team Rocester in the final of the Leek Cup with a magnificent Micky Elliott hat trick.

Sadly the team disbanded in the 80s, but a few dedicated ex-players re-formed the club in the 90s. There were more victories. They won the Marsden League Cup, walloping Abbey Hulton Suburban Club 5-0 in the final with a Simon Snape hat trick. Next came the clubs first ever Sunday Premier Championship - they became Marsden Premier League Champions.

I remember an incident in about 1997. We drew Ipstones in the Congleton Cup and they said they were going to put Brown Edge in their place. We were big rivals. Well we beat them 5-0. They weren't very pleased and this chap started on the referee, Mr Castile. Mr Castile said *'Look they've outplayed you - they've beaten you and I'm making a report about your conduct'*. Well this player lashed out at Mr Castile and broke his jaw and cheekbone. I remember he drove himself to the hospital. A typical referee, he sat there completely calm. It was only on the insistence of the Brown Edge officials that the police acted on it. It was on local Midland news.

A few more honours were received before the village lads achieved the finest honour to date. They won the Staffordshire Football Association Trophy Cup. 138 teams entered from Stoke-on-Trent, Stafford, Walsall etc. In the final the Edge beat the favourites, Ball Green WMC 4-1, with goals from Paul Cumberlidge, Simon Snape (2) and man of the match Martin Lear. When team Captain Dave Haycock lifted the Trophy Cup, the Edge became the first team of the Leek and District Sunday League to win the highly prized cup. To date no other team has been able to match the achievement.

This long list of honours should make us proud of our village team, Brown Edge Football Club ('Achievement by endeavour').

Today's Team - Kevin Bagnall (manager)

The present Brown Edge team have had a very good season, reaching two cup semi-finals and finishing third in the Leek District Sunday League.

The team feel that having a pitch on Brown Edge instead of having to play all their home games at Leek would help them in their efforts to win more honours - and generate more support.

We are hopeful that the Parish Council will be able to help in finding some suitable land.

YMCA Reserves team.
Back row: Roy Cotterill, Ivan Redfern, Ken Basnett, E Cunliffe, S Slack, R Dawson, Billy Dale.
Front row: Arnold Hancock, R Taylor, Derek Berrisford, Fred Rolinson, Eric Slack, R Berrisford.

YMCA - Leek and Moorlands League champions 1953.
L-R: ?, ?, Jack Rushton, C Goldstraw, Derek Berrisford, ?, Mrs Tipper, Arthur Proctor, Sam Bratt.

The League Cup 2nd Division Championship 1955/6.
Back L-R: Ray Durber (Sec.) Jack Rushton, Martin Healey, Bill Mountford, Arthur Trueman, Ray Simcock, Bill Rushton.
Front L-R: Ron Dawson, Cliff Johnson, Derek Berrisford, Tommy Holdcroft, Derek Berrisford, Johnny Hancock.

Presentation Dance for the above at Leek Town Hall.
Front L-R: Johnny Hancock, Mabel Durber, Ray Durber, Nora Rolinson, 7th Ray Simcock.

1968/9 Back row L-R: Phil Docksey, ?, David Condliffe, Tony Moss, Kevin Reynolds, David Elliott,
Front: ? Butch, Barry Snape, ?, ?, Jim Baker.

BELOW:
1972/3 Runners up in Leek and Moorland's League 1st Division.
Back L-R: Anthony Taylor, David Condliffe, Tony Hollinshead, Roy Snape, ?, Ken Tate, Wilf Goodwin, Dave Elliott, Mr Graham Baker with trophy, Colin Sherratt, ?, ?, Tony Moss (Capt.), Stephen Willis, Kevin Reynolds, ?, John Riley, Mr K Murfin, E Chadwick, S Stanway.
Front: ?, ?, Barry Snape.

BELOW:
Brown Edge FC c1965.
Back: Tommy Moore, Jess Pew, Anthony Pew, Ken Dawson, Bill Mountford, Ray Brown, Ken Tate, Alan Hilditch, Tom Jones.
Front: David Crossley, Ray Goodwin, Graham Mitchell, Tony Spragg, Tony Taylor.

Easy for 'Edge

Ash Bank Utd 1
Brown Edge 9

PDSL outfit Ash Bank United gave Brown Edge FC a warm welcome to their new pitch at Chell for this pre-season friendly last Thursday evening.

It was the first friendly in which the Edge fielded a strong side. Four players scored twice, brothers Craig and Simon Snape, Craig Morris and new signing Julian Pomelli while his brother Justin Pomelli scored the ninth.

Brown Edge were boosted by the return of goalkeeper Paul Smith and he was rarely troubled in a match which turned out to be a one sided affair with Simon Snape's dazzling wing play creating a number of chances for strikers Julian Pomelli and Craig Snape.

Julian was in fact unlucky not to complete a hat-trick, a third effort was ruled off-side.

Lyndon Evans, Paul Rigby, Trevor Owen and Graham Gibson on the other hand were in control at the back for the Edge.

That victory was followed up by a win over Durham Ox on Sunday.

Edge hit 21!

Brown Edge FC 21
The Priory 0

THIS was the first meeting between the two clubs and as the score suggests it was a very one sided affair.

Simon Snape brushed aside his father's club record of eight goals in one game as he hit the back of the net a creditable ten times.

The Priory started the game with some tight marking but this was soon over come by the Edge's flowing football, and Snape raced in to the visitors box to start the goal feast.

Priory seemed overwhelmed as they watched the score build up in the first half to ten goals.

At the restart Priory made changes and worked hard at containing the Edge, but another eleven goals hit the net in the second half.

Along side Snape's ten, where Daniel Berrisford with three, Mark Sherratt recorded his first hat trick for the Edge, substitute Daniel Snape grabed two, Darren Owen and Rob Wright got one each, with an own goal making up the final score.

Despite the score, both teams showed alot of respect and sportsmanship.

Man-of-the-Match: Simon Snape.

BELOW:
Brown Edge FC c1998. Staffs. Association.
Challenge Trophy Cup.
Back row L-R: Craig Snape, Paul Cumberlidge, Barry Snape, Martin Lear (Man of the match), ?, ?, Paul Simcox, Lee Bourne, Daniel Berrisford, Roy Snape.
Front row L-R: Simon Snape, Justin Pomelli,?, ?, Capt.Dave Haycock, ?, ?.

1973/4 Back: Roy Snape, Jim Baker, Dave Condliffe, Colin Leek, Colin Ward, Philip Dutton, Keith Myatt, ? .
Front: Barry Snape, Ken Tate, Vincent ?, Paul Parr.

Bagnall team c1959. Back: Keith Ashman, Malcolm Sims, Bob Hassell, Jackie Barrett,
Dave Berrisford, Graham Mitchell, Harry Turner, John Rushton.
Front: Derek Bourne, Malcolm Cox, Ken Bedson, Jimmy Berger, Ken Dawson.

Barrie Scott - Upper Stonehouse Farm

I was born in the West Midlands in Smethwick, in 1931. My parents were Winifred and James Scott. We moved to Upper Stonehouse Farm at Brown Edge in 1952. Dad had no experience of farming. He had served in the First World War, then during the Second World War my parents had their own factory making Bailey bridge end posts. After the war they kept a general store and later a fruit shop. When I left school I went to work on a fruit farm at Little Witley near to Worcester. After there I went to a big arable farm near to Brewood, then got a job as farm foreman at Shareshill.

When we decided to buy a farm, to farm as a family, we looked around a bit and Upper Stonehouse was one that we could afford. It was 45 acres and we bought it off Richard Wood. The owners before that were Holdcrofts who had a baker's shop in Burslem. We have been told the farmhouse dates back to the 1660s and that they used to hold church services here before the church was built. We believe it was possibly built for a son of the family living at Lower Stonehouse, another very old farm. The stone would have been quarried from down there.

Holdcrofts modernized the house. The stairs went straight up from the big living room so they put a hall in. They also had a bathroom installed and built the dairy. There is a door in the living room that leads down some steps to the old well.

When we moved to the farm we decided that the pasture and meadows weren't very good at all - they were worn out. We decided to grow corn first and then re-seed the area after to improve it. We bought the stock already on the farm. We'd got about ten cows which were milkers, and we had four breeding sows. We also had 500 hens which we used to keep in the loft above the cows in the big old barn which is still there. We sold some eggs private but most of them went to the grading station of the Milk Marketing Board. They were collected once a week. Hodgkinson's Dairy at Stoke used to pick the milk up at half-past eight.

A local fellow used to bring his boar to the pigs and we took the weaners to market at eight weeks old. We grew potatoes on a couple of acres and about the same amount of kale, which was used for stock feed. Turnips were already in the fields when we came. Haymaking was done with a Ferguson tractor and mower. It was a Ferguson 20 then we swapped it for a 35. We cut about ten acres for hay. We started doing some silage later on and put it in a pit in the barn up yonder, in a stack.

When it came time for threshing the corn, Charlie Sidebottom used to bring his threshing box. The neighbours used to all gather round when we were threshing at our place and then we went to a neighbour's farm and helped them. The job needed about five or six of us. Harold Shufflebottom had already cut the corn for us with a binder and then we stooked it up in the field. We carried it in when it was dry and then the box came and threshed it out. It knocks the corn out and bales the straw. You ground the corn, made a mixture and fed it to your cows. It saved you buying food. The straw was used for bedding for the stock. The lady of the house had a lot of potatoes to peel as a lunchtime meal was always provided for the workers.

Haymaking was always a busy time on the village and we enjoyed a drink of beer when we'd done. One year my wife Doreen and sister-in-law Elizabeth went up to the top pub, the Rose and Crown, to get the much needed liquid refreshment. They came back empty-handed as it was closed and a notice outside said 'Sorry no beer'. They were sold out because of all the haymakers - a pub with no beer!

We had some help on the farm. Stan Davenport worked for me full-time for a while and

SERVICE FOR ROGATION SUNDAY AT UPPER STONEHOUSE FARM.

The corn stooked up in the field.

Barrie's mum and dad James and Winifred
Scott with the hay cart.

Barrie on his tractor, with
brother-in-law Brian
Lawton behind.

Clive Simcock did part-time. My brother-in-law, Brian Lawton, helped at weekends. I started to help out with doing contract work for other farmers - ploughing and muck spreading and all that sort of thing. The small farmer's scheme was introduced where they got a subsidy to improve their farms, by ploughing and re-seeding. I used to do a lot of work up in the hills t'other side Leek; then John Meredith, a forestry contractor, appeared on the scene one day. He was looking for someone to plough some land at Baddeley Green for tree planting, so I did that. The next thing was they were making Tittesworth reservoir so John put in a price and got all the work for the tree planting and fencing, so I went and did the ploughing for that.

We decided the money I was making at the contract work was better than farming. Dad had died in June 1961. We had sold some of the stock and had just kept the cows, now I was contracting. One Sunday morning one of the cows, Blackie, was missing. I'd never counted 'em the night before when I'd fastened them up. I had to do the milking because the milk lorry was coming so I asked Doreen to see if she could find the missing cow. She went down the field and sure enough it was upside down in the ditch and was dead as a nit. It had been trying to reach for some grass and had slipped. It was our best cow that we'd had for years - it always happens to the best. It had only calved a fortnight before. Doreen was very upset and that was the straw that broke the camel's back.

We made the decision to pack in farming. We found a house in Woodhouse Lane, Biddulph, and put the farmhouse and land up for auction in April 1965. We tried to sell the whole lot but couldn't get the price for it. However in the August Proctors came and offered for the farm. They didn't really want the house for themselves, they were going to let it, so we agreed they could buy the land and we would stay in the house.

We've said many times that it worked out for the best - it wasn't meant to be. This was our family home; we brought up our children, Janet and Andrew, here and have always been very happy living on Brown Edge.

The Hodgkinson family outside Upper Stonehouse, early 1900s.
L-R: Harry, Hannah, John, Hannah (mother), James (father), Annie, John, c1905.
On the 1843 Tithe map this farm is shown as Woodhouse. It was also called Top Stonehouse.

Harvest Supper in the mid 1950s.
Back: Jesse Jolley, Maggie Hargreaves, Margaret Hargreaves, Beryl Cook.
Front: Miriam Hargreaves, Rev. Attoe, Mrs Clements, Winifred Scott, Annie Willett,
May Shufflebottom, Beattie Holdcroft, ?.

N.F.U. Harvest Supper at Norton Community Centre late 1960s
L-R: Reg Clements, Jack Machin, Ethel Machin, Doreen Scott, Barrie Scott, Mrs Sergeant, Mr Sergeant.

A guard of honour for Reg Clements and his new bride, leaving St.Anne's Church.
Supporting the bale of straw are L-R: Mrs Unwin, Mrs Sergeant and Doreen Scott. Janet Scott is on the far right.

Garden Party at the Vicarage, late 1960s.
L-R: Anne Jolley, Winifred Scott, Doreen Scott, Margaret Clements and Jesse Jolley.

Dorothy Simcock née Lowe

I was born at The Coppice Farm, at Hill Top, in 1919 where we were in lodgings. My parents were Frederick and Kate Lowe. Mother's maiden name was Morris and she came from Alton. While I was still small we moved into accommodation at Greenway Bank Farm, near Knypersley Pool. Robert Bailey farms there now but his grandfather, John Bailey, was there then and he was more like a grandad to me. My brother, Bill, was born at the farm. Dad was a miner then but helped on the farm as well.

A cottage came vacant at Hill Top and so we moved back there, where I stayed until I got married in 1941. It was the middle one of Chapel Cottages, opposite the Rose and Crown. The cottage actually belonged to my great grandmother, Joyce Lowe. She was my dad's grandma and I was named Dorothy Joyce after her.

Grandma owned all 3 cottages and lived in the end one, but we still had to pay her rent. She was very strict. Mother used to leave me brother and I with her every Friday while she went to Burslem. We had to sit all the time on a wooden settle, and my word we had to sit still. I remember the 'uxter' cart, which is like a horse and float, used to come. He sold fruit and veg and we were allowed an apple.

Mother used to walk to Smallthorne, then catch the tram down to Burslem. Later the buses started - Mr Horne had one, Turners did Hanley, Jim Berrisford up Old Lane had one and also George Mayer - but they'd all got different routes.

Great Grandma Joyce Lowe.

My dad was lovely and he used to take me everywhere as Mother was busy with my baby sister, Gertrude. I always remember going with him to the cinema at Milton and it was silent pictures. We were very happy. He used to work at Black Bull, down the mine, but it was hard work and there were no baths then. He'd come home and Mother would have the fire going in the kitchen, heating the water to fill the tin bath.

I was only about 11 when Dad died in 1931. He'd been coughing for a while but he got pneumonia. The neighbours were very good - you know people in them days always rallied round. Rob Dawson's dad used to come and sit with Dad. In those days they waited for the crisis, they didn't go into hospital and there were no tablets to help.

Mr Berrisford, Jacker's father, was good and Mrs Berrisford was very kind to my mother. Bob Lomas, Gordon's uncle -

The family on Marshes Hill c1929.
Mum and Dad with Gertrude, Bill and Dorothy back right.

Dorothy, Gertrude and Bill.

BELOW:
Dorothy with a lovely big bow
Mum and Bill c1921.

Chapel Cottages, at Hill Top, snowed
in on 21st January 1941.

Thawing a little. Alice Mayer on the
left and Kate Lowe.

I can see him now sitting by the bed. I remember they laid straw on the road in front of the house, so Dad wouldn't hear the horse's hooves when the carts went past. I went to Holdcrofts to sleep at night and my brother, Bill, went to Mrs Berrisfords. My sister wouldn't leave Mother.

The vicar of Endon, Rev. Pavey, used to come. We were in Endon parish then and he'd walk up. Dr Hurd came and stayed with me dad and Dad died while he was there.

Mum was left with 3 young children and she was very poor. All Mother had was a guinea a week - it was 10 shillings for herself, 5 shillings for me and 3 shillings each for me brother and sister. She had to pay for everything out of that.

We all helped in the house. Mother always did the black-leading of the grate on a Friday and Saturday morning. I had to clean the floors on my hands and knees. It was also my job to do the dishes but Mother would help. My brother had outside jobs to do, like cleaning the toilet, which was a wooden tub type outside. He used to scrub the toilet seat and make such a good job it was nearly white.

Later Mother went out scrubbing and cleaning. She used to go to Lane Head Farm, Holehouse Lane to Mrs Yarwood. When the Yarwoods moved to The Gables at Endon she went there. It's a nursing home now. Mother was very quiet but everyone got on with her.

On Sundays Mother always went to St Luke's Mission at the top of Broad Lane. We went to Charlesworth's Mission (Free Mission) morning and afternoon and then at night we had to go with mother to St Lukes. Elsie Rowland's grandparents looked after St Lukes Mission. Although it was small it was nice. There was a little altar and reading desk and we sat on wooden chairs with rush bottoms.

They used to have lay readers from different churches. Mr Harrison from Clay Lake used to come a lot. The vicar from Endon used to come once a month for Holy Communion. We were all confirmed there. I remember Elsie Rowland used to come with her mother every Sunday evening and walk from Lask Edge, pushing a pram with her brother Vince in.

Dorothy's confirmation 1933.

Dorothy and friends at Hill Top c1932. Back: Edith Lomas, Dorothy. Front: Gertie Lowe, Vera Lomas, Dorothy Lomas.

There was a little wooden shop by St Luke's Mission kept by Violet Higgins, but there was no end of little shops. Mrs Proctor had one in the Colliers Arms yard. Lily Foster had a shop at the end of Top Chapel Lane and my brother-in law, Harold Simcock, had one in Chapel Lane.

I was friends with Ethel and Nora Dawson who lived at the Colliers Arms and I was also friends with Ivy Berrisford who lived at the Rose and Crown. Mrs Berrisford used to say to Ivy and me, *'If you'd like to mop the tap room floor I'll give you 6d.'* We were glad of that. Mr Berrisford had a lovely garden and during the war he built an air raid shelter there, for us all to use.

I used to walk down to school with my friend Edith Lomas. I liked school, I was never outstanding but I got through. We went to the new infant's school until we were seven. Miss Garner was the headmistress and there was Miss Hollins and Miss Jenkins. I remember Miss Garner teaching us a poem called 'The Miner' and I can still remember it today.

> Under the ground the miner goes
> Where sunbeams never peep.
> He works away, by night and day
> And sometimes while we sleep.
> His safety lamp he keeps alight
> Its little steady glow
> Seems like a spark down tunnels dark
> To show him where to go.
> He's tired and weary when day is done
> As homeward bound he'll go.

In the big school Mr Jones was the headmaster. He was very strict, as was Miss Dawson, and even out of school we had to behave. The boys had to touch their caps - there was respect then. Mrs Jones, the headmaster's wife, was a lovely person, she really was.

I remember one day, in the big school, we were congregating and chattering away and Mr Jones came out of the schoolhouse where he lived. *'If there isn't less chattering and talking there will be weeping and wailing and gnashing of teeth.'* It went that quiet you could hear a pin drop.

We had assembly every morning with prayers and a hymn, and sometimes Rev Lawton would come. There was trouble if anyone was late. Mr Benton was very good with music. I remember Mr Benton used to lodge with Holdcrofts, at the start of Back Lane, Hill Top. He would give me 6d a week to carry his lunch to school for him. I thought it was wonderful having 6d you know. He knew we were poor and was just helping us.

My brother worked a lot in the school gardens and he's always liked gardening. We girls went in the garden as well, doing weeding and sweeping the paths. We had needlework and cookery with Miss Dawson and oh how we were taught! There was no electricity so we cooked on an enclosed type of oven fitted over 3 paraffin heaters. We did pastry and also made rock cakes. We iced cakes at Christmas time.

We were taught how to wash and starch. We had to bring some socks from home and were shown how to rub the foot part clean. Of course they were home knitted socks in those days. We also learnt how to patch and repair. We were all very poor but they were happy days

When it was the miner's strike in 1926, we used to go up to the school on Saturday mornings. We would sit outside the school on straw mats, and Mrs Hargreaves and Mrs Hodgkinson used to come round with baskets giving out egg sandwiches. We also had little containers of Jacko malt, which was like ovaltine and had to be mixed with milk or water. We were also given these during the school week as well.

I left school in 1933 when I was 14 and went into domestic service. I went to live in, and work for some people called Hallem in Station Road, Endon, next to the chapel. It was the Manse House actually and the family rented it. They had two boys, John and Michael. I was what they called a general servant and they were very good to me. I was allowed to go home on Wednesday and Sunday afternoons after I'd washed up.

I used to walk home with my friend, Edith Lomas, who also came from Hill Top. Edith was in service at a house in Orford Road, which was at the back of Hallem's house, where I worked. When I was upstairs cleaning we used to wave to one another with a duster - how you remember little things like that.

Our mothers washed our uniforms for us. The morning uniform was a blue dress, a big white apron and a white mop cap. After I'd done all the work and washed up the lunch dishes, I had to go and get washed and changed into a black dress and little white apron. I then had a little white cap that went round my head and was threaded with black velvet. The white cuffs on our dresses came off for washing and starching.

I had to get up at 6 o'clock and the first thing I had to do was to peel an orange and cut it into quarters and take it in to the two boys. Then I took Mr and Mrs Hallem a cup of tea and started getting breakfast. They always had a full cooked breakfast.

I was very happy there and was very sad when they couldn't keep me on. Mr Hallem worked in insurance and they said I deserved a higher wage, but they couldn't afford to give me any more. I was only getting 5 shillings a week, which I gave to my mother and she gave me 1 shilling pocket money.

I moved to a place in High Lane, Burslem; I didn't live in but went daily. There was a mother, three daughters and a son and they were all in the teaching profession. I was very happy there too and was working there when war came.

When I was 21 I married Joseph Simcock from Chapel Lane. They lived in a cottage opposite the chapel, now called Willow Cottage. Joseph's father was known as Little Jess and they had 10 children. I met Joseph when I went to Leek May fair with Ivy Berrisford - he was with Ivy's brother, Jacker. The fair was held in the old cattle market, where the bus station is now. Joe was working in farm service at Bradnop and living in so I hadn't met him before

Later Joe got a job collecting milk from farms for Forsters at Tarporley in Cheshire. The housekeeper there had left and the chap said I could go and have her job after we were married. Joe was already living in. We got married in 1941 and this is what we did.

I was married at Endon Church in a borrowed dress, and we had a little tea after in St Luke's Mission. Relatives came from Alton and we went back with them and that was our honeymoon. We walked to Endon station and caught the train to Leek, then caught one to Alton with all these aunties and cousins. We stayed at Auntie's house for 3 days and that was that. Still they were happy days.

When I had my call up papers we came back to live at Brown Edge and I went to work on munitions at Swynnerton. We rented a house next door to Harold Simcock's shop in Chapel Lane. At

Dorothy's husband Joe with his milk lorry outside Chapel Cottages 1940.

Swynnerton I was capping bullets and I had to work shifts but I didn't like it. It was an awful job, but I didn't work there long as I became pregnant with my son, Alan. I later had three more sons - David, Brian and Eric. I would have liked a little girl but they've all been very good.

In 1948 mother met up with Mr Johnson who lived at Bluestone Farm. It was opposite Bluestone Cottages. It isn't there now; it's been knocked down. Mother had been a widow for 18 years and Ernest Johnson had lost his wife. They got married and were very happy.

When the war was on my husband, Joe, had to choose whether to go in the army or down the pit and that was when he became a miner. I think it was 1958 when he had this bad accident - buried at Norton Colliery. It was on a Sunday morning and I was at home and I'd got two of the children with measles. Someone came from the colliery to tell me and to take me up to the hospital.

Joe had broken both legs and had head injuries. The neighbours were very good.

Dorothy with her sons: David, Brian, Dorothy, Eric and Alan.

He was in hospital for a very long time and he was never the same after that. He had to go to Betley Court for rehabilitation to get him to walk again. He never did a full time job after - they got him part time work on the Bank at the colliery

Outside Bluestone Farm. The Johnson family were the last to live there. It belonged to the Water Board and was demolished in the 1970s. Dorothy, Betty Marshall, Kate Johnson (Lowe), Lizzie Spink and David Simcock.

We moved to a bungalow in Cheddleton near to my sister. It was easier for Joe and had just enough garden for him but we'd only been there 18 months when he died. I was alright though because I'd made a lot of friends. I moved back to Brown Edge in 2000 and am very happy here.

BILL LOWE - THE SCHOOL GARDENS

The school had a large garden, the headmaster, Mr Walter Jones being a keen and knowledgeable gardener. A Mr Stony, who used to write a gardening column for the Sentinel, was a regular visitor. About half the garden was divided into plots, which were available to school leavers for night classes. Mr Jones got the seeds in bulk, thereby cheaper, having regard to the widespread unemployment at the time. The produce from these plots was a welcome subsidy to many family budgets.

The entrance to the garden was through a small gateway from the girl's playground, and just inside was a notice board on which was written:

> Kiss of the sun for pardon
> Song of the birds for mirth
> You are nearer God's heart in a garden
> Than anywhere else on earth

About halfway up the garden a lily pond was made, and this was fed from a spring in a neighbouring field. In the bed of the water supply route were carved the words: 'Books in the running brooks'. Two fair sized stones, at the side of the pond, had flat surfaces, and chipped on to them were the words - 'Sermons in stones' and 'Good in everything.' Mr John Benton, a teacher, directed the carving, and he had obviously acquired some expertise in this art from his father who was a professional carver of memorial stones.

In the school garden, c1931. Back: Ada Weaver, Ethel Unwin, Edith Lomas.
3rd row: Dorothy Dabbs, Rene Sherratt, Dorothy Lowe.
2nd row: Edith Harvey, May Grindy, Ellen Beardmore.
Front: Lottie Holdcroft, Vida Ellis, Lizzie Heath.

It was a demonstration by Mr Jones where I first saw a tomato plant grafted onto a potato. It was planted in a box with a glass front. I always remembered it.

On a different note, Hill Top had the distinction (if that is the correct word) of providing two brothers (both Grenadiers) as poll bearers at the funeral of King George V. They were Joe and Bill Hancock and I understand this is the only time this has ever happened. Sadly both these chaps failed to survive Dunkirk.

Philip Rushton

I was born on Christmas Eve in 1938 in St Anne's Vale. My father, Jack Rushton, was actually born in Smallthorne in 1915 but he moved to Brown Edge when he was about twenty, living in High Lane just below the Post Office. Dad's parents were Bill and Maud Rushton and they had two sons, Bill and Jack. Although Grandad Rushton was a miner at Norton colliery he kept both of his sons out of the Pit. Uncle Bill went as a potter and Dad was a knitter at Wardle and Davenport in Leek. Dad used to be a member of Smallthorne Church and was in the choir. He later joined Mum's chapel at Hill Top and became an enthusiastic member of their choir.

When he came to Brown Edge Dad was soon attracted to my mother, Dorothy Bailey, who lived on a smallholding called Rock House, built by her Great Grandfather William Hargreaves. She lived with her parents, Martha and Albert Bailey and her sister Alma and brother Jack. Mum was born at Rock House in 1915 and she lived in St Anne's Vale all her life, as I have.

Grandad Bailey was a shot firer at Norton and Whitfield collieries but, as with a lot of the miners at that time, he supplemented his income by running a smallholding. Mum went across

Philip's mum, Dorothy, age 18.

the road to St Anne's school and when she left at 14 she went working at Sandbach's clothes shop in Burslem. It was quite a prestigious shop at the time, in St.John's Square. As she was a pretty girl she used to do a bit of fashion modelling there as well.

Mum and Dad got married on Christmas Day 1937 at Brown Edge church. Dad purchased a piece of land from his father-in-law and had a house built, High Tor. A bungalow was built next door which was occupied by his parents, Bill and Maud Rushton.

In 1940 Dad was conscripted into the armed forces and he actually served abroad for six years from October 1940. He was in North Africa, followed the North African campaign across and went to Sicily then on to Italy and Greece. They got bogged down in the battle for Cassino. At the end of the war there was trouble in Yugoslavia so they shipped them out there, and he didn't actually get back to Brown Edge until April 1946. This is my first recollection of Dad because he left for the war when I was a small toddler. He had had no home leave.

I recall my neighbour, Frank Mayer speaking to me: *'If you go along to School Bank and meet the bus, a soldier will get off and that soldier will be your father'*. So this is what I did, feeling a bit bemused and excited. The bus was one of Brown's charabanc buses with wooden slatted seats and Dad was still in his soldier's uniform with his kit bag on his back.

I remember the reception for him wasn't at High Tor but at Rock House, where Grandma and Grandad Bailey lived. The family all collected at the top of the yard as my father and I came from the bus. That was my first recollection of Dad, as a seven year old. My sister Anne was born in 1948, so there is ten years

Philip's dad Jack Rushton 1945. 89th Battery 23rd Field Regiment Royal Artillery.

between us. Dad wasn't away for ten years but I think it took him a long while to get his breath back!

Grandma Maud Rushton with her 2 sons, William on
the left and Jack on the right, c1925.

BELOW: Firemen at Norton Colliery, c1930.
Back 2nd right Grandad Albert Bailey.
Seated: 3rd Joe Mayer, 7th John Proctor.

The family outside High Tor c1946.
Philip, Dorothy, Jack & Clive Proctor (cousin) at the front.

During the war years, although I was living at High Tor, I spent most of my time at Rock House on the smallholding with my grandparents. We had quite an idyllic war really. The Germans dropped no bombs and I can never remember being short of food because of the smallholding. There were pigs, a cow called Judy, hens and other domestic animals.

The family owned the field opposite, in front of John Powell's cottage. I remember Judy giving birth to a calf there and the dustcart men going to give her a hand. I also remember Mr Harrison coming up to butcher one of the pigs for us, in the backyard of Rock House. On the small field where my Auntie Gladys Bailey's bungalow is was the site of the cow house and the pigsties. On the roadside was the Smithy. I never knew it to be working but it had a cart house and then upstairs there was a room with a big old grindstone.

The long field by the school, where the Willows is now, was also part of the smallholding. Family rumour has it that this land used to belong to the church and was exchanged for the wood just behind the vicarage, which was the family's.

From St.Anne's School I went on to Hanley High School and then joined Stoke-on-Trent City Police as a cadet in 1955. I think I must have been impressed with Reg Twemlow, the village bobby. He lived in the police house near Brownhills Road and was here for quite a while. I think it was Bobby Evans before. Reg was a very respected man on the village. He also found time to write poems and had some published. He interviewed me and then two or three years later, as a constable in Stoke-on-Trent, I would meet with him on the County boundary between Ball Green and Ridgway. I was based at Burslem and we had no motor vehicles or radios, just a few pedal cycles. The only police cars were in the city centre at Hanley.

Reg used to come pedalling on his bicycle from Bemersley and I would meet him and pass over messages and envelopes and things like that. Policemen in those days had to ring in from phone boxes at set times to receive messages. Things have changed just a bit!

When I joined the police you lived in police houses and that meant that they could move you around as and when they wanted. Then, as Stoke-on-Trent was a small area, 9 by 4 miles, they found it was cheaper for officers to own their own houses and give them a rent allowance.

It was fortunate that some land came for sale next to High Tor when I was looking for a house. My father bought it initially and passed it on to me and I had a house built. Jean and I moved in when we were married in 1964. In the police I served in the Stoke-on-Trent and North Staffs area so there was never a need to move. Brown Edge is quite a delightful place and nice to come back to at the end of the day

After the war Dad returned to his occupation in the mills at Leek, doing early and late shifts. He was always very active with the YMCA and the building known as the TAB was now across the road from Rock House. He was a member of the team who replaced the old wooden YMCA building with a more substantial ex-army camp, brick structure. I remember them erecting it, all local men. The two concrete buildings were joined with a connecting door. As you went in there was a full-size billiard table in the first hall and a kitchen and toilets. The big hall was used for dances, cubs, W.I.etc. It was open every night except the Sabbath, of course.

Dad liked playing table tennis and billiards and was involved in the football team there. He was a keen footballer. I enjoyed boxing but not football - I had two left feet. The team were in the Leek and Moorlands team and attained many honours. Dad followed that until he was about 45, when he decided that captaincy of the football team was perhaps something he ought to give a rest. He was always involved in the TAB though, doing secretarial duties, treasurer and other duties.

A YMCA table tennis
presentation.
L-R: Derek Berrisford,
Derek Fox, Roy Cottrell,
Ian Adams, ?.

Jack Rushton with friends, c1935.
Back: Albert Sherratt, Bob Cumberlidge.
Centre: ?, Jack, Fred Scarlett.
Front: Bill Cumberlidge, Tom Basnett.

BELOW: Snooker in the TAB.
Jack Rushton about to break.

The Parish Council at the opening of the cemetery June 1984.
Back: Clive Proctor, Harry Slack, Jack Rushton, Alan Turner, Philip Durber, Ken Meredith.
Seated: Colin Simcock, Elizabeth Tatton, Peter Turner, John Bourne, Arthur Watkins, Susan Watkins.

The official opening of the new Working Men's Club late 1960s.
L-R: 1st Jack Rushton, 3rd Mannie Slater, 7th Rev.Rastall.

BELOW: The last meeting of Leek RDC. 1974.
Centre: 4th Herbert Bourne, 10th Jack Rushton. Seated: 1st Harry Hammond.

I remember Grandfather Rushton used to caretake there. My friends and I used to practice table tennis, snooker and billiards and hope to reach the standard of people like Roy Cotterill and Derek Berrisford, who were noted experts. Ginger Williams was good too. They played in leagues and they used to win - they were bloody good!

I think young lads weren't any better behaved then but there was more respect for elders probably. Facilities were provided and you'd got somewhere to go. If you did step out of line you could expect a smack around the ear, whether it was from your parents or whoever was looking after the YMCA at the time.

When Father's generation were getting past it to run it, no one in my generation wanted to take it on so it was sold to Staffs County Council, as a youth club and run by them. Dad was on the management committee then but it had its good times and

bad. The building was demolished and a bungalow now stands on the site.

Father was a very forthright character - he called a spade a spade, as demonstrated in an incident with our neighbour, Dickie , and his hens. Dad did a lot of vegetable gardening and these hens kept getting into his back garden and stealing the peas. He'd warned Dickie face-to-face, man-to-man, that he was to keep his hens under control, but obviously he hadn't and eventually in frustration Dad said to him *'Look Dickie, if you don't keep these hens up I'm going to shoot'em.'* Dickie said he would clip their wings, etc.

A few days later I remember lying in bed at High Tor early one morning when I was awakened by an almighty bang that caused the house to quake and shudder. It was in fact Dad firing the shotgun through the back bedroom window towards the vegetable garden. He'd apparently been woken up by the clucking of hens stealing his peas, and no more to do, he'd rushed downstairs, loaded the shotgun and blown Dickie's hen to smithereens. Not being a sneaky person, the same day, when Dickie came to collect his eggs, he was greeted by Dad holding this mutilated hen. *'Here you are Dickie, I told you what would happen and here's the hen.'* There was an icy atmosphere for some time after.

A few years before Dad decided to hang up his football boots at the age of 45, he decided to stand for the council. He was elected in 1952 as a Labour member on the Leek Rural District Council. He was also involved in the Textile Worker's Union and served them for many years. Leek R.D.C. then seemed to be run as a council representing the village rather than a political party. Dad had friends and colleagues in other parties. Later there was an amalgamation of councils and the R.D.C. was abolished and went into its present form as Staffordshire Moorlands District Council. The new council was run on more political lines which didn't sit very well with some of the members. You were expected to sit in a particular place (Labour or Tory). I think what rubbed the old fellow up and besides being told where to sit, being told how to vote and what to vote for. He was called before the Labour party and was sacked, so he continued on the District council as an Independent member. He continued to be elected until he retired in 1987, and Philip Durber took over. He was honoured with the chairmanship of Leek R.D.C. in 1965/66.

Dad was involved with the Brown Edge Parish Council since its formation and in 1987 he took on the job of parish clerk. He pushed to have the new cemetery done, and there were a lot of negotiations. It took a long, long time.

After his adventures abroad with the army Dad never again left the shores of Britain. As with most soldiers he never talked about his experiences. He rarely spent a night away from his home in St.Anne's Vale. Although he was

Jack outside High Tor 1997.

not born on Brown Edge, he loved the village, and his involvement in its daily life became his all consuming hobby. He had a contented and fulfilling life.

Mum died in August 2000 at the age of 86 and Dad followed soon after, in March 2001, also aged 86. They are buried in the new cemetery, not far from their beloved St.Anne's Vale.

Irene Daniels née Shawcross

I was born in 1943 in Baddeley Green nursing home. I was nearly born in Chapel Lane itself as Mum had to walk in labour to the bottom of the lane, clutching the wall, because Nurse Mountford wouldn't bring her car up. She said it was too narrow. I lived at Church View until I went away to university at 19.

I went to the infant's school at Brown Edge for two years then on to St.Anne's juniors. Mrs Powditch was head of the infants and then there was Mrs Williams. Mrs Powditch was very strict and I was a bit frightened of her. We had a good grounding in the three 'R's.

There were four classes in the juniors and the head was Mr Fisher. Arthur Berrisford, a Brown Edger, taught there and Phyllis Davenport took class three and I was terrified of her. Miss Davenport was

Irene aged 3, at Church View with Flo Simcock.

a friend of Mum's and we used to visit her for afternoon tea, but she gave me no favours. She lived in a cottage in Church Road. She was a terrifying teacher. I also remember Miss Green and later Mrs Proctor. They were all very strict and stood no messing about.

Later Mr Brown came and he was very popular. He had a wonderful sense of humour. I remember we used to have a third of a pint bottle of milk each day and we would collect the tops for making pompoms. I went home every day for dinner, but when Mum became a dinner lady I had to stay for dinners and I hated them.

We had assembly every morning and the local vicar came in regularly. There was a large picture of Jesus at the front of the big hall. I

The dinner lady team at St.Anne's School, early 1950s.
L-R: Annie Shallcross (Mum), Annie Willett, Elsie Charlesworth.

remember there was a stove in Mr Fisher's class and when it was very cold a fire was lit and we sat on the floor around it for lessons. There used to be a huge pile of coke in the playground.

My social activities were mostly associated with St.Anne's Church or Hill Top Chapel. I went to Sunday school at the chapel from about three, I think. I loved it. We had tiny chairs and used to sit round the piano and sing. Enoch Simcock and his wife, Connie, ran the Sunday school. All the children loved Mr Simcock. The highlight of the year was the Anniversary when all the children sang on the stage. Each year we progressed to a higher level on the stage and everyone waited desperately to reach the top seating. I never achieved it as Mum decided it was time for me to go to St.Anne's Church, where all the family were members. I was upset as I had to make new friends.

Mum and Dad, Arthur and Annie Shallcross (née Cumberlidge)   Irene with her cousin, Philip Cumberlidge, at Church View.

When Rev Attoe was vicar there was a drama group and I was involved as Mum loved the plays. I acted in some but was always nervous of forgetting my lines. The plays were held in St.Anne's school and a proper stage was erected and we had curtains, props and music. It was a very popular event.

All my mother's family, the Cumberlidges, were very involved in church matters. I always went on Sunday school outings and the bell ringers' trips. We looked forward to them. There used to be film shows in Sandy Lane, but I was never allowed to go to those

The highlight for me was the church fete. In those days it was a church activity whereas now it is a village affair. Mrs Hammond was in charge of the queens and she asked Mum several times for me to be queen, but I refused. I had no confidence but I did agree to being in Barbara Heath's retinue. In those days we paraded on carts, drawn by horses, belonging to local farmers. When I was involved the fete was held in the school playground, but one year when my cousin, Pam Cumberlidge was queen, it was held in the vicarage garden. Refreshments were served from the vicarage kitchen and stalls set out on the lawns. Mr Lansdale was the vicar then and I remember being allowed to explore in the vicar's wood, high up behind the gardens.

I enjoyed the fete most of all when it was held in Hargreaves field, where the cemetery is now. There were marquees and all manner of entertainments, including swing boats one year I remember.

One year it was decided to present purses of money to the Church of England's Childrens Society. The venue was the Royal Albert Hall in London. I was chosen, along with others, to present a purse to Princess Margaret. It was a very big occasion as it was the first time I had been away from home and my first train journey. Rev. Attoe accompanied us and we stayed in a hotel. I remember being excited about riding in a lift, a very memorable weekend. Rev.

ABOVE:
St. Anne's Drama Group staging *Mrs Wiggs of the Cabbage Patch*
Back: Teddy Wright, Leah Crossley, Elsie Bourne, Bill Bourne, Mrs Mountford, Madge Bond, Bert Pointon, Tom Mitchell, Mrs Frank Proctor, Betty Jolley, Richard Turner.
Front: ?, ?, ?, Hilda Proctor, ?.

LEFT:
Drama Group with *Lilies of the Field*
Back: Teddy Wright, Mary Harvey, Nora Baddeley, Bert Pointon, Mrs Mountford, Hilda Proctor, Betty Jolley, Tom Mitchell. Front: Billy Bourne, Mrs Frank Proctor, Elsie Bourne.

BELOW:
Brown Edgers at leisure in the 1930s.
Back: Madge Tomkinson, Bill Hollins, Winnie Hollins, Fred Scarlett, Doris Cumberlidge, Bob Cumberlidge.
Front: Tom Hollins, Annie Cumberlidge, Bill Cumberlidge.

Attoe was a bubbly, larger than life character who had exciting ideas and things buzzed at church during his incumbency.

Outside school and church I had what I look back on to be a very rich village life. There was a lot of friendship and community spirit. People helped each other. Most of my friends lived in Chapel Lane, Hill Top and Fiddlers Bank. During school holidays we spent time roaming over Marshes Hill, looking for bird's nests and building dens.

I remember taking a bottle of water and some jam sandwiches, meeting up with a group of children, and wandering down to the feeder at the bottom of Tongue Lane. We'd sail pieces of wood under the bridges and wait for them to come out the other side. Mum always said, *'Be back for tea'*. We had no watches but knew the time by our hungry stomachs

I spent a lot of my early years on farms. Uncle Jack, Mum's uncle, lived at Hobbs House, a smallholding then. When I was little I used to walk down Chapel Lane each morning with Grandad Cumberlidge who lived with us. We got a can of milk from Hobb's House and it was warm when it went in the can, straight from the cow.

One of my best friends was Doreen Unwin who lived on a farm behind Marshes Hill - Burnfield's Farm. I spent hours there. Haymaking was special. We were allowed to ride on the hay, piled up on a trailer, as it was taken in from the fields. My friend's mum made herb beer especially for haymaking time, as it was thirsty work, and we were allowed some - a great treat.

I think most Brown Edge children loved the winter prospect of sledging for which there was plenty of scope. Children local to Chapel Lane depended on me to get permission from Uncle Jack Cumberlidge at Hobbs House, to use his fields adjacent to the lane. He was a grumpy man so I dreaded knocking on his door for permission. He always said yes grudgingly, insisting we shut the gate when we'd finished. One stone gatepost is still there now, where the entrance to the fields was.

Sledging down those fields is one of my favourite memories, despite getting wet, cold and suffering later from chapped legs. Dad made me a sledge with shiny metal runners, but it went down the slope so fast I landed under a wire fence near the infant's school, and cut my legs. Dad removed the runners, much to my disgust. The fun of sledging was to have the fastest sledge. He deliberately made my next one heavy and it was a nightmare mauling it back to the top of the slope. After a while we used to go home to get warm and change our clothes. Then we were back out again. We also made slides down the lane if it was icy, but sometimes Dad put ashes on from the fire, saying it was too dangerous. We used to slide all the way from the chapel, down New Lane and on to School Bank.

In those days we had no car so we spent a lot of our time walking and visiting friends and family. We used to visit Mum's Uncle Tom at Bemersley and walk there and back. My paternal grandparents lived at Mow Cop and we used to visit every other Sunday. We walked to Black Bull and caught a bus from there or, if the weather was bad, it was three buses - Brown Edge to Burslem then one to Tunstall and then one to Mow Cop. It took more time getting to places than the time spent there. They were big events these days out.

This was the era before supermarkets so we used the small village shops for our needs. Towards the bottom of Chapel Lane was Harold Simcock's shop and I remember going there with Mum with ration books. My Uncle Joe was the proprietor of Cumberlidge's shop in Church Road and we had a weekly order delivered on Fridays. Uncle Joe also had a catering business and when I was at Westwood I used to help him on Saturday. I used to love it and got paid five shillings.

Joe Cumberlidge's catering team.
L-R: May Hargreaves, Hilda Worthy,
Eileen Sherratt, Annie Shallcross, Joan
Berrisford, Doris Hollins, Elsie Rowland.

RIGHT: Mum retiring as school
dinner lady 1976.
Centre group: Joy Tatton, Paula
Mitchell, Joan Ball, Annie
Shallcross, Rev Moseley, ?, John
Ellis (headmaster), Harry
Hammond.

BELOW:
Wedding of Bob and Vera
Cumberlidge 1943 (Mum's brother).
Bridesmaids Winnie, Iris and Beryl
Foster. The boy is Philip Foster.
Behind Bob are Mum, Dad and Joe.
Seated left is Mrs Foster. Brenda
Foster is standing far right.

The Lump of Coal, with the Sheldon family, early 1900s.
Irene's great grandfather, Richard Sheldon, was licensee from 1862 until 1909.

We would walk down Hough Hill bank on Friday mornings in school holidays, to buy fish from Mrs Berrisford's fish shop and meat from Harrison's butchers. We used to get cakes from Mrs Crossleys, which is now the paper shop. I think the cakes were baked at the back of the premises. We used the cobblers, Tommy Jones and Mr Winkle was at the Post Office. Another shop opened on School Bank and was run by Mrs Charlesworth.

One of my favourites was Mrs.Beresford's chippy. Each Friday, on our way home from school in Leek, my friends and I would call in to buy threepence worth of chips to eat as we walked up Hough Hill. We saved the money out of our dinner money as our Mums usually gave us extra if they hadn't got the right change. Sometimes we hadn't enough to buy chips, but Mrs.Beresford took pity on us and filled paper bags with batter bits which were free. Friday afternoons were worth waiting for.

Mum also liked to patronize door-to-door salesmen as living where we did in Chapel Lane, these deliveries were welcomed. Frost's van used to arrive with all manner of ironmongery and Albert, the driver, always had time for a cup of tea! We had bread and milk delivered. Mr Clements Snr. delivered the milk in those days. Mum was a knitter and sometimes a man called Harold Shallcross used to arrive with a huge suitcase full of skeins of wool. He came from Biddulph and was a chatty friendly man, again always grateful for a cup of tea. I had the job of helping Mum wind the skeins into balls. I used to place the skein over a chair back. I hated the job as it made my arms ache!

Brown Edge was very different in the 1940/1950s. Chapel Lane itself had few homes. There were a few stone cottages, less brick-built houses, and the Methodist chapel. A few farms were scattered about and many open fields. There were six public houses. There was the Lump of Coal, once owned by my great grandfather, Richard Sheldon. Dad used to like a drink at the Collier's Arms at Hill Top, although I only remember him going Saturday nights.

When I was in my late teens Dad bought his first car, a Morris Traveller and then he and Mum would go further afield on Saturday nights.

In my teenage years the highlight was the YMCA in St.Anne's Vale, locally known as the Tab. Arthur Sherratt played drums and put records on. So popular were Thursday nights that people came from Norton, Norton Green, Ball Green, Baddeley Green etc.and as far as Leek. A few Brown Edge people married people they met at the YMCA hop. Members of the committee supervised and provided refreshments. In later years we went to Leek Town Hall and the Queens in Burslem.

Every village has its personalities and in my teens I was chuffed to know Brian Oakes of Brown Edge. He started up a pop group called 'Bry Martin and The Marauders'. I think he was the lead singer. They played in the Tab and Leek Town Hall and other venues. I think he was on the television once, in the Comedians.

Another personality was the cricketer, David Steele, who lived down High Lane and was in the junior school when I was there. He was BBC Sport's Personality of the Year in 1975. I had never seen him in person again until he opened the village fete in 2004. I accompanied my mum, Annie Shallcross, who crowned the queen that day and I enjoyed reminiscing with him over refreshments. He had wonderful and amusing memories of the village.

Mostly everyone knew everyone in Brown Edge. Families married into other local families but sometimes married out of the area. My Dad came from Mow Cop. It was only when the miners'

Bob and Vera in the garden of their home in Chapel Lane on their silver wedding anniversary 1968.

houses and council houses were built that Brown Edge expanded. People came from Durham and Northumberland to work in the mines here. There were also quite a few Polish people who settled in the area after the war.

Brown Edge has grown, with bungalow estates and plots of land being developed, but I still feel the village is quite unique and still boasts a real community spirit. To me now, as an observer who hasn't lived in the village for over forty years, it seems that newcomers to the village have integrated well and taken on the village ethos.

Mum on her 90th birthday.

FETES, FAIRS & FUNCTIONS

St.Anne's Church Queen Paula Mitchell 1976. Back: Harry Hammond, Gladys Hammond, Janine Leese, Mandy Snape, Irene Daniels, Paula, Pam Upson, Louise Harvey, Tracy Condliffe, Rev. A Moseley,
Centre: Lesley Basnett, Jane Hackney, Angela Fenton, and Angela Knox. Front: Andrea Webb, Joanne Lowe, Jane Leese.

Lane Ends Coronation Party in Church House 1953. Back: Graham Mitchell, Ann Morris, Roy Hargreaves, John Fenton, Beryl Selby, Wallace Turner, Gladys Hammond, ?, Gladys Bailey, May Fenton, Matty Foster, Rose Mitchell, Vera Tomkinson, Meda Beardmore. Centre: Pauline Tomkinson, Michael Tomkinson, Malcolm Mitchell, Barbara Holdcroft, Lorraine Holdcroft, Glenys Mitchell, Danny Holdcroft, Alan Beardmore. Front: Susan Bailey, Peter Dawson, Elsie Morris, ?, Rosemary and David Attoe, John Holdcroft, Gwyneth Hammond, Pat and Christine Worthy.

St. Anne's Church Queen Barbara Heath 1950.
Members of Barbara's retinue on the platform were Irene Shallcross, Margaret Pointon and Mary Holdcroft.

St. Anne's Church Queen, Shirley Tate, 1972.
Shirley is pictured with attendants Diane Gabri and Susan Ash.

Annie Shallcross when she opened Brown Edge Fete in 2004.

Margaret Bourne as Sandy Lane Chapel Queen, 1950. Back: Lila Goodwin, Yvonne Cooper, ?, Yvonne Weaver.
Centre: June Bourne, Ann Adams, Pauline Turner, Christine Berrisford, Pauline Weaver, Maureen Weaver.
Front: Brian Mountford, Sheila Condliffe, Audrey Harrison, ?, Janet Woodward, Alan Holdcroft, Carol Walmsley, Pat Walker, Keith Morris.

St.Anne's Church Queen Julie Lear 1971. Julie's retinue: Mark Tate, Jane Durber, Jane Fox, Julie Walker, Jackie Lowe,
Ann Stonier, Caroline Beardmore, Janice Forrester. Behind is the 1969 queen, Janet Scott, with her retinue.

Fairfield Avenue Coronation Party 1953 outside the home of Jack and Ethel Farrington.

Snow White and the Seven Dwarfs (or is it eight?) Standing: Hilary Mathews, Judith Berrisford, Anne Rushton, Veronica Snape, Lynn Foster, Julia Tyler, Susan Bailey, ?, Pam Cumberlidge, Clive Turner. Kneeling: Brian Lancaster, Paul Harvey, Valerie ?, Sheila Gladwyn, ?. Sitting: Pamela Mosedale, Steven Meadowcroft, Irene Foster, ? Lancaster, Susan Holdcroft.

ABOVE:
Brown Edge Dramatic Society
- *Storm in a Big Cup*
L-R: Madge Bond, Mrs Mountford, ?,
Hilda Proctor, Leah Crossley,
Mrs Wright, Joe Cumberlidge.

RIGHT:
Fashion Show at Hobbs House c1968.
L-R: Winifred Scott, Doreen Scott,
Diane Lawton, Elizabeth Lawton,
Margaret Parkinson, ?, ?, ?.

Harvest Supper, with apple pies.
Back: Jesse Jolley, C Bourne,
Betty Mosedale, Mrs Willett, Mrs
Richards, Mary Holdcroft.
Front: Beattie Holdcroft, Mrs
Clements, David Jolley, Mrs
Clews, Gladys Lowe.

St Anne's Church queen,
Alison Mosedale 1973.
L-R: ?, ?, Antony Bedson,
? Pomelli,? Baker, Alison,
Paula Mitchell, David
Fenton, Mandy Snape, ?.

BELOW:
Julie Lear and her retinue
with spectators c1972.

BELOW:
St Anne's Drama Group
- *Mrs Wiggs of the cabbage patch*
Back: Joe Cumberlidge,
Gladys Hammond, Rev. Attoe,
?, Hilda Proctor, Madge Bond,
Bert Pointon, Leah Crossley, ? ,
Betty Mosedale, Richard Turner,
Tom Mitchell.
Centre:
Teddy Wright, Bill Hollins, Bill
Bourne, Mrs Frank Proctor, Mr
Hall, Mrs Mountford, ? .
Front:
3rd Rosemary Attoe.

The Carnival at Willfield Farm early 1970s.
Pamela Mosedale on the right wearing a spotted dress. Her Dalmatian won the prize for 'dog most like its owner'.

St Anne's Church Fete in the school playground. Note view of New Lane before the houses were built c1970

Some of the volunteers at the commencement of the Village Hall project 1988. The old St Anne's C of E School was opened as a village hall (1st stage) by Joan Walley MP in Dec 1997.
Back: John Basnett, Graham Bonser, ?, Dougie Frost, Arthur Watkin, Barrie Scott, ?, Malcolm Dawson, Brian Lawton, Linda Lea, ?, ?.
Centre: Edith Bonser, Janet Sims, Merle Harvey, Janet Scott, Doreen Barnes.
Front: Emma Sims, ?, Doreen Scott, Brenda Basnett, Dee Townsend.
Centre: Vicky Turner, Barry Simcock, Samantha Turner.

BELOW:
Sandy Lane Chapel Queen Sheila Slater 1955.
L-R: Elizabeth Paddock, Veronica Lythcoe, ?, Diane Cooper, Billy Cockburn, John Baker, Sheila, Hilary Mathews, Clive Turner, June Bourne, Shirley Simcock, ?.

Some of the well dressers 2007.
L-R: Margaret Fernihough, Hilary Shaw, John Shaw, Dorothy Hibbitt, Doreen Barnes, Adrian Mason, Elizabeth Lawton, Lesley Hulstone, Gary Lovatt, Jane Walters, John Lawton, Elizabeth Tunnicliffe.

RIGHT:
St. Anne's Church Queen Elizabeth Charles with Rev. Attoe 1954. Members of the retinue were June Hancock, Pauline Turner and Rosemary Attoe.

BELOW:
The Over 60s on holiday.

Sandy Lane Chapel Queen
Pauline Weaver.
Back: Margaret Bourne, Pauline,
Lillar Goodwin.
Centre: Mavis Harrison, Pat Walker,
?, Janet Heath.
Front: Tony Slater, Pauline Snape, Peter
Worthy, Judith Hewitt, David Cope.

A social occasion in the new
Sandy Lane Sunday School
building early 1960s.
Back: 5th Mrs Thickett, 6th
Mrs Richards (vicar's wife).
Centre: Mrs Heath, Iris Turner,
Mrs Slack, ?, ?, Pat
Rutherford, ?, ?.
Front: 5th Mrs Berrisford, 6th
Debbie Simcock.

Sandy Lane Chapel Queen Margaret
Bourne 1953.
Back: Christine Wilcox, Margaret,
Jean Sutton.
Centre: Janet Woodward, Sandra Beff,
Veronica Lythcoe, Susan Walker.
Front: Keith Tanner, Sheila Slater,
Jeffery Simcock, Sheila Bourne,
Phil Gratton.

St.Anne's Church
Queen Hilary Mathews
1960.
Back: Steven
Meadowcroft, ?, ?,
Hilary, Veronica Snape,
? Crossley,
Paul Harvey.
Front: Susan Holdcroft,
Pamela Mosedale.

Sunday School party with the
Rev. Rastall 1971.
Back: Jackie Snape, Diane
Cooper, Graham Hudson,
Peter Whiston, Martin Oakes.
Centre: Julie Snape, Pamela
Bartlam, Jill Stevenson,
Christine Taylor, Glenys
Hewitt, Shirley Tate.
Front: Alison Starkey, Mandy
Snape, Mark Tate, John
Wedgwood, ?, ?.

Hill Top Chapel Queen
Jill Shufflebotham 1977.
Jane Wardle is on Jill's
right.

Betty Mosedale née Jolley

I was born in 1929 in Lane Ends. My father, Jonah Jolley, was born on Brown Edge and was part of a large family. My mother, Elizabeth, lived on a farm at Berryhill and was one of nine children. I believe they met at a friend's wedding.

My father bought the house in Lane Ends on the tram between Burslem and Smallthorne, from a Mr Boult, a Burslem businessman. At the beginning of their married life Dad's grandfather, Daniel Holdcroft, lived with them. Dad's father was Joseph Jolley but I never knew him. He died in 1899. Dad served in France during World War 1 in the Lincolnshire Regiment and his sister Alice served as an army nurse.

Four generations c1913.
Daniel Holdcroft, daughter Mary Basnett (formerly Jolley), grandson Jabez Jolley and great grandson ?.

Betty's mother, Elizabeth Jolley, c1915.

Dad was a miner during his early years and returned to the Pit after the war, but after a bad accident he set up a workshop at the end of the house. He made shoes and clogs, the machines being driven by a stationary engine outside. He was kept busy as almost all workmen and children wore clogs and new 'tips' were constantly needed.

My father later became a Brown

The house in Lane Ends.

Betty's dad, Jonah Jolley.

Edge postman. On school holidays I often walked with him on his delivery round which not only covered the village but the outlying houses and farms as far as Lask Edge and Knypersley. Later he moved to Norton where he delivered the mail by bicycle. He continued at Norton throughout the Second World War, working split shifts,

Dad as the postman, delivering to Norton.

First World War group. Jonah Jolley is on the back row 5th from the left. His sister Alice Jolley is seated 2nd right.

Afternoon tea outside Bleak House c1910.
L-R: Zillah Jolley, Jim Basnett, Dinah Jolley, ?, Mary Basnett (nee Holdcroft), Daniel Holdcroft, Alice Jolley.

Mum and Dad's wedding 1916.

involving sorting, delivery and collection. There was even a delivery on Christmas morning!

My mother had a small shop, firstly in a smart wooden shed beside the house, but later in what had been my father's workshop. She sold all the basic foodstuffs, many kinds of sweets and chocolate, and she also had a large cabinet of patent medicines, bandages etc - anything that might be needed for coughs, upset stomachs and grazed knees.

Elizabeth Jolley outside her shop.

Mum also sold hen corn. At the outbreak of war I remember a delivery man from the wholesalers bringing into the shop a large sack. *'I didn't order corn'* was my mother's response. *'This isn't corn, Mrs Jolley, it's gold dust!'* he replied. That 'gold dust' was sugar, which was packed away in the storeroom and shared out amongst her customers as 'extras' on special occasions.

Rationing was not easy. Cheese was the greatest problem as cutting and shrinkage often meant there was nothing left for the family. Worst of all was counting the monthly 'coupons' and making returns to the Food Office in Leek. I wonder if they ever checked! Any mistakes were threatened with imprisonment! Brown Edge escaped many of the rigours of rationing. My brother Eric and I were registered rabbit keepers, rearing rabbits for food. Country people were very enterprising and there was always a chicken, rabbit or even a joint of kid (our neighbours kept goats) to supplement the meagre meat ration. With patience the top of the milk could be 'churned' to make a little butter.

Before the war our pleasures were very simple. There was so little traffic we could play football and cricket on the 'bank' using the stone stumps as wickets or goals. Two horse-drawn carts often put an end to the games - Boyce Adams, the grocers from Hanley, delivered bread, the horse having his rest and feed while Mr Harvey visited his relatives for a cup of tea, and the other was the ice-cream cart. We could hear his bell, giving us time to gather our coppers. Our dog was so fond of ice cream that he once jumped into the cart, giving the man a scare

Storms seemed to be more spectacular in those days. Our house was once

A group outside the Infant's school, c 1934.
Back row L-R: 2nd Ashley Jervis, far right Eric and Betty Jolley.
Front row L-R: 1st Stanley Baddeley, 5th Ronald Charlesworth.

St Anne's School with headmaster Billy Jones c1900. Back L-R: 5th Jonah Jolley.

struck by lightning. A small fireball ran along the cable from the aerial, through the window frame, shattering the glass, along past a picture, removing all the gilt, and blowing up the wireless. It then went on to the plug, which was reduced to fragments, dropping to the quarry floor where it rolled through the open front door to earth itself in the garden, leaving a burn mark in it's wake. We all sat mesmerized, my father picking shards of glass from his face while I sat under the table with the terrified dog.

We were able every year to have a seaside holiday either in Rhyl or Blackpool. Clarence Nixon used to take us as he was the only neighbour with a car. This all stopped on September 3rd 1939 when war was declared on what was to be the first day of our holiday that year.

Every year between the wars Brown Edge held a carnival. It was called Hospital Saturday and the aim was to raise money for the hospitals. This was before the NHS. In about 1935 Belle Hodkinson was chosen as queen and I was one of her attendants. It was exciting to take part, but more excitement was to come. All the carnival queens gathered at a special event in

Hanley Park c 1935. Elsie Ashley the retiring Hospital Queen hands over to Belle. Betty is front right.

Hanley Park where Belle was chosen to be Hospital Queen for the coming year. And an exciting year it was, full of daytime and evening events. It was the first time I had been photographed with ladies and gentlemen in evening dress.

Wartime left some unusual memories, teams of Air Raid Wardens spending their evenings fire watching. One group met in our shed. I well remember when they changed shifts at 2am; they would knock us all up to assure us that all was peaceful.

My school life passed relatively peacefully. I first attended the recently built infant's school where Mrs Powditch was head, with Miss Hollins looking after the new little ones. I remember starting to school when I was four, then catching all the childhood infections and my mother being told to send me again when I was five. My memories of the 'big' school are somewhat vague. Mr Walter Jones was in poor health and coming to the end of his headship and big changes were taking place.

One of my earliest memories was celebrating the Coronation of George VI. We all dressed up and paraded round the village before enjoying sports on Singlet House field. Those of us who had gardens big enough built bonfires to celebrate at home. Every year we celebrated Empire Day. All the school children gathered on School Bank. The Union Flag was raised and we all sang patriotic songs conducted by the Headmaster from Church House balcony.

Perhaps my most abiding memories of school days during wartime were under a new headmaster, Mr Jennings, when the school had to accommodate the evacuees who were billeted in many homes. The school day was divided into two 'long' halves and so part-time lessons were the order of the day. The evacuees and their teachers occupied the school for half the day and the local children and teachers the other half, changing about each week. On the sessions not in school we were taken for walks by Miss Phyllis Davenport, often to Knypersley and the Trent valley. The sun always seemed to shine!

I remember in May 1945,when I was a pupil at Orme Girl's School; we were celebrating Founders' Day. All the girls walked through the quiet streets to St.Giles Church but after the service what a different town it was. People everywhere smiling and putting up flags and bunting. *'Haven't you heard '* they called,*' the war is over'*.

After school, college in London and two years teaching, I returned to teach at St.Anne's Junior School under Mr Eric Fisher. There were four classes, Miss Phyllis Davenport, Mr Arthur

Confirmation group outside the Vicarage c1945. Betty is on the back row next to Rev. Ramsden.

Berrisford and Miss Betty Jolley (me), all 'Brown Edgers'. It is unusual for the entire staff of a village school to live there. Mr Fisher was the last headmaster to live in the School House. A happy time. I have fond memories of the really nice, well-behaved children of that time.

One sad memory lingers. An assembly was called unexpectedly mid-morning on a grey February day. Rev. Attoe, who was a regular visitor to the school, came to break the news that George VI had died and we now had a Queen.

I was married at St.Anne's Church in 1954. The church was being completely re-decorated for the first time for many years. When I looked in on Friday afternoon you can imagine the scene - scaffolding, ladders, sheets, paint cans and workmen everywhere. The foreman came over, '*It's looking lovely, isn't it? it will be even better when we've tidied up. There's a wedding tomorrow!*' There was indeed - it was mine.

After my marriage I left Brown Edge with my husband Denis, to live in Congleton.We returned a few years later after buying Hobbs House Farm, spending a considerable time re-building and renovating the house and buildings.

I returned to teaching. Mrs Powditch was still Headmistress with Mrs Williams (Harriet Hollins) but because of an increasing roll a third classroom was needed and there was a temporary building in the playground. The school had its own kitchen. Mrs

Wedding of Betty and Denis 1954.

Baddeley was in charge and Mrs Dawson supervised the children during lunch and afterwards.

In recent years a church queen has been crowned at a fete to raise money for St.Anne's Church. The parents of the queen and her retinue then work to raise even more funds for the church. Our two daughters, Pamela and Alison have both filled this role, so money raising became a habit. The Spire Splash was a sponsored swim to raise money for the repairs to the church spire. All ages took part on a lovely sunny afternoon. Then professional models helped

The Spire Splash at Hobb's House 1969. Betty and Denis are standing left. Marjorie Johnson is swimming on the left.
Seated by the pool L-R: 3rd Pamela Mosedale, 7th Paul Harvey.

make a fashion show a successful money raiser for the Church queen's effort. Every room in the house was packed. There were the usual coffee evenings, wine and cheese parties, and during the summer a tennis tournament for the more athletic (or foolhardy) of the community

Charities were not forgotten. We held a bonfire party for Heart Research. Blaster Bates lit the bonfires and John Sutton supervised the firework displays. On warm summer evenings, we opened the pool to the local children. They each made a small contribution to charity (Cancer Research) and enjoyed a couple of hours swimming and lazing in the sunshine.

Brown Edge has changed a lot over my lifetime. Lane Ends has been changed to Church Road. Our old house, two other cottages and Joe Cumberlidge's shop were demolished for the road widening and other properties lost much of their front gardens. The allotments are no more and Singlet House Farm has been swallowed up by the estate of bungalows

A Wartime Evacuee

Early in the war children from Manchester were evacuated to Brown Edge, among them the three Harrison children, Bernard, Ernest and Sylvia. In the 1990s I met Bernard on School Bank. He was retired and back in Brown Edge with his wife on holiday, re-visiting old haunts and friends of 50 years ago, remembering his school days at St.Anne's and particularly the great kindness afforded to him by Mr John Benton and his wife. They took him into their home until he could be found a more permanent one with Mr and Mrs Berrisford in Job's Pool.

He remembers Mr Sherratt who lived at the top of Thelma Avenue, the Machins, Harry and Mary, the Foster family, Miriam and Hazel Pointon, the Johnson family who kept the shop, the Bibbey family from Lane Ends, the Banner family from Woodhouse Lane and happy memories of the Weaver family, Mrs Weaver in particular who helped him with his schoolwork. Although Bernard left school still unable to read and write, he remedied this by his own efforts. He went from farming to landscape gardening and then to estate management at Hilton Gravel Headquarters. He is now retired and living in Stalybridge.

St. Anne's Infants School Class party c1960.
L-R: Winnie Baddeley, Betty, Addie Dawson, Harriet Williams, and Mrs Powditch.

Stanford Charlesworth

I was born in 1938 in Chapel Lane. My grandfather was Ralph Charlesworth whose father, John formed the Free Mission at Hill Top. Ralph had three sons, Eber, Jack and my father, Wilf. When he was a lad Dad lived at Bluestone cottages, and then at some stage moved to Chapel Lane. The family lived in three adjoining cottages in Chapel Lane and I was born in the middle one - Hillcrest. My mother was Elsie Yardley before she was married, from Norton Green.

Stanford aged 3.

Although they weren't builders, the three sons, Eber, Jack and Wilf, built a bungalow for Grandfather on land opposite the cottages. It was called Roselyn and the garden was quite steep, but there was a little bit of flat, with just about enough room to put a tent on. I remember one summer me and Philip Rushton camped out the whole of the school holidays in my ex-army tent. If it was cold we used to get up about 4 o'clock and go on the bikes across Chapel Lane and Marshes Hill. Grandfather lived in the bungalow with his second wife, who we always knew as Granny May. I remember she always had these fantastic hats, especially when she went to chapel. They had like fruit dangling off - apples and bananas hanging from the side - very impressive!

Grandfather Ralph Charlesworth.

I had to go to chapel three times on Sunday - Sunday school and afternoon and evening service. I've never been that way inclined but I wouldn't have missed it for anything. There was nothing else to do. I love music and play the organ at Biddulph Church and I think that's come from being at the mission. They used to have a quartet there - Wallace Turner's dad, Fred, sang base, Uncle Eber sang baritone, Uncle Jack sang tenor and my father sang the top part, falsetto. I think they sang at Lichfield Cathedral and places like that. The lads, me and my cousins, Norman and Ron, used to laugh about them and call them the 'Inkspots'. On Anniversary Sunday some folks couldn't get in and used to have to go back home. We used to sing things like 'We are going down the valley, going down the valley, going down the valley one by one' -I can't remember any more. It was a traditional Methodist service, like a hymn sandwich - a hymn, a prayer, a hymn, a lesson, a hymn, etc.

Charlesworth brothers outside the Mission at Hill Top.
L-R: Wilf, Eber and Jack.

Uncle Eber was the most religious. I've heard it said if Eber was on a bus, and if any of the

The interior of Charlesworth's Mission (The Free Mission).
An inscription on the pulpit read:
'Sacred to the memory of Frederick Lowe who was a member of
this church for 35 years, died March 14th 1938, faithful unto death'

LEFT:
Grandfather Ralph Charlesworth with his 3 sons.
L-R: Jack, Ralph, Wilfred (Stanford's father), and Eber.

Young members outside The Mission with Jack, Eber and Wilf. The children are Eric and Joan Rowland, Linda Harvey,
Peter Charlesworth, Jenny Foster, Marion Lomas, Annette Sheldon, Joseph Sheldon, Joy Scarlett, Wendy Scarlett, Jillian Harvey,
Shirley Brassington, Margaret Fox and Angela Brown.

passengers were swearing, he would get off. He would get things that were called texts, which were little leaflets with quotations, a drawing or photograph or whatever. When he went for a walk and came to a stile he would wedge one of these texts somewhere, hoping someone would find it. He always wore a dicky bow and he was the one that played the organ. Dad was the conductor and Uncle Jack was the treasurer. All three brothers worked at Whitfield. When Dad left school at 11, until he was old enough to go to Whitfield he farmed at Meir's farm, in Broad Lane. He never worked underground at Whitfield but on the Bank, and later in the Stores.

My father had violin lessons and all the family had American organs - the ones that you pedal with your feet. Every house had got one, how on earth we got in our little living room. We'd got a big table in the middle and a great thumping sideboard, and then they'd got one of these great big radiograms and an American organ that went halfway across the wall. Dad loved his classical records.

At the chapel I used to stand at the side of this organ with this big handle to blow, and there was a length of cord with a lead weight on, and you had to keep this between two marks. If you were getting tired and you didn't blow it would slow down and Uncle Eber would shout out *'Blow, blow!'* Uncle Eber used to show off a bit and part way through playing the last verse he'd close his book and play the rest from memory. Well, Grandfather was known for repeating the last verse if he liked the hymn, and many a time he'd start off singing the last verse again. Uncle Eber had to try and find the hymn again as he'd closed the book.

I remember some of the local preachers we had we used to laugh our socks off at. We always sat on the back row. The Free Mission, also known as Charlesworth's Mission, closed in 1963. The three brothers were getting old. Jack's son, Ron, had died, Eber's son, Norman, was living in Wales, and I was married and living in Biddulph. There was a bad winter in 1963 and it meant they had to keep going up through the snow, to keep the boiler going in case the pipes froze. When they closed the chapel all the contents went to other chapels.

When I started to school my mother went to work in the office at Bullers and then she did a job as a collector for Pearl Insurance Co. She'd got no car but went collecting at Ball Green and she did it for quite a while as she enjoyed it. She later got a job at St.Anne's School when they opened the kitchens and she did dinners there until she was 65.

1949 Mr Fisher with his prefects at St.Anne's School.
Back: Malcolm Chadwick, Terence Heath, Ken Turner, John Bourne, Stanford, Alan Taylor, Maurice Heath.
Front: Alice Haydon, Margaret Lovatt, Alice Holford, Glenys Hancock, Nora Proctor and Sheila Hammond.

After Dad died in 1991 Mother used to go on the bus to her old Zion chapel at Norton Green, where she came from. She was hail and hearty and died just before her 90th birthday. She used to do the Sentinel crossword every night and she'd always ring me up and say *'Can you give me a word for so and so?'*

Stanford 1948.

I went to St Anne's School and I remember one morning, when we were in the infant's, the air raid siren went and we had to go straight into the air raid shelter, which was between the two schools. At the big school there was Miss Berrisford who was later Mrs. Durber, but the one that everyone was frightened to death of was Phyllis Davenport. We used to have hymn singing in the hall and her favourite expression was *'You're singing like guttersnipes!'*

The head, Mr Fisher, was a good bloke - I've got happy memories of that school. It was like a culture shock when I went to Leek High School. It was the custom for every lad on the first day, where the washbasins were, to have his head stuffed under the tap. After the first day I got home and I didn't want to go again!

When children were off school we'd be gone all day down the fields - Knypersley Pool and Lion's Paw. We'd make all our own enjoyment - tree climbing and jumping brooks - they were great days. We used to swim across Knypersley Pool from one side to the other. I remember once when we were down there, on the Friday of Stoke wakes week, a lad got drowned. We were all swimming together and someone came running across the bank and said someone had drowned. He was a lad who couldn't swim and he went in the water near the tower. He came from Ball Green. The shore goes straight down there and he was out of his depth in no time. I remember, before we got home, word had reached Chapel Lane that a lad had been drowned. Well my mother knew I'd gone there swimming and she was worried silly.

We used to get a lot of snow and Hughie Winkle and me always went sledging. We would sledge from the top of Winkle's field, where the trig point is, down the field and through a gateway on to the end of Chapel Lane. We'd sledge down a set of steps and all down New Lane, and if we'd got enough speed up we'd cross over in front of Marion's shop, down Boardman's Bank and finish up at the farm down the bottom. It was a long walk back!

I remember on Halloween night in the 40s and 50s I used to go 'guising' with some of the other children along the lane. We would go from house to house singing songs and knocking, hoping to be given a few pence to buy fireworks with. There were no pumpkins or dressing up in black - we went round as we were, probably carrying a candle in a jar to light the way. This is one of the songs we used to sing:

> I have a little moneybox under my arm.
> Two pence or three pence will do it no harm.
> Sixpence or a shilling will do it some good.
> The best little money box made of wood.

I remember when the plane crashed over Broad Lane. I was six and Alice Holford, Hughie Winkle and I were picnicking up Jakes Bank, what some of us called the spot where the trig point is. We saw the plane come right over and gradually getting lower and we saw it crash. It was the biggest fire I've ever seen - smoke must have gone up in the air hundreds of feet.

It was an American Liberator four-engine bomber. When they realised the plane was in trouble they must have started jettisoning fuel. Jim Holdcroft, at Knypersley Mill, noticed that his lorry was covered with it. The plane came over Knypersley cricket ground. It had hit a tree and the pilot managed to get it down in the corner of the field between Wood Bank and Painter's field. We went running down the lane but only went as far as Broad Lane. The crew got out and the police arrived on the scene and the RAF.

The wreckage was there for a while. They removed the main part with a big long RAF loader - they used to call them a Queen Mary. For years after there was a part of that field that nothing would grow on and it's where all the hydraulic fuel had run out and settled. There were still tiny bits of wreckage all over the place. My father had some melted valves and he had them in the shed for years.

When my cousin, Norman, came out of the forces in the early 1950s he came back on the bus one Sunday night. He'd been in Singapore for all his National Service time. I met him and I struggled up New Lane trying to carry his case for him. I was that thrilled to see him.

Norman was keen on biking and by that time I'd got a drop-handled bike. I was about 15. I'd got a day off school and we set off on our bikes and cycled from home to Chester, then on to Birkenhead. We went through the Mersey tunnel to Liverpool and we came back through Warrington, Knutsford and Congleton. All that in a day! When we got to New Brighton we sat in a shelter on the prom and I was so tired I just fell asleep. It was a long day!

We used to play cricket and football for hours on School Bank and we used to have to pack in when Brown's bus came. We also played on Marshes Hill with Derek Fox who played in goal for the YMCA team. The team used to play up Broad Lane and had a good side, with some real characters. When they played away, me and Philip Rushton used to go with them on Harry Hammond's 'Bluebird' bus. Ian Adams was a good footballer, and Derek Berrisford and the Knight brothers.

I remember when I went to the Mission we used to have an outing every year. The first one we went on was on one of Sammy Turner's very old buses and the outing was to Congleton Park. We ventured further afield after that. We always had a day out on Whit Monday. Harry Hammond got rid of his 'Bluebird' and had an AEC, something more modern. We were all on the back seat and the bus broke down. All the men had to get off and push but we didn't - we got down behind the seat!

There were a lot of characters up near Chapel Lane in my day. There was Florrie Wright who they called Black Diamond. She lived across Back Lane. There was a bloke who lived in an old caravan over the top from the highest point. He was called Mo Flick - I don't know why. Alfie Simcock and his family were called Tottys and they lived in an old place. In a cottage opposite Hill Top chapel was a Mr Simcock who they called Little Jesse. He was only about 4' 8". He'd got a bit of an entry and the boys' footballs always used to go down. We used to run down and get the ball and Little Jesse would come out, he always had a stick and he used to wave it and say *'Ar'l swape thee feght from under thee!'*

When I was 18 I was called up to do my National Service and I did 2 years in the RAF. I went on the train to Cardington near Bedford where we were kitted out with our uniform. We did our 8 weeks square bashing in West Kirby on the Wirral then I went to Kidbrook in London to learn my RAF trade, which was air movements. My final camp was at Lyncham where I did 18 months until I was de-mobbed. It was a fantastic 2-year experience and I feel it's a real pity they don't do it today. The discipline was good and it was real character forming.

When Dad was retired and I was living at Biddulph he used to carry a few tools in an old bag and walk all the way from Brown Edge, through the fields to Woodhouse Lane in Biddulph. He'd do a few jobs for me and then I'd run him home. He was very fit. He never smoked and he never drank. He was 89 when he died.

THE BARRAGE BALLOON (Norman Charlesworth)

In the early days of World War II I attended St.Anne's School. We heard in school that a barrage balloon was flying high over our village and sure enough, as we came out of school, we could see it high up over Old Lane. We rushed up in great excitement to the top gardens of the Simcock family.

The balloon was secured by its trailing wire to the Simcock's clothes line post. Someone said the army had been informed and were coming to re-capture the balloon, which had broken free from Crewe. The local bobby was in attendance to make sure everything was in order.

The excitement grew and so did the wind at this bleak spot, the trailing wire stretched like a fiddle string and, with an explosive sound, away soared the balloon, taking part of the post with it. We ran after it cheering, only to see it disappear over Marshes Hill. We heard later the balloon had tangled with an oak tree at Rudyard and its day of freedom was over.

EVENTFUL MEETING LED TO THE FORMING OF FREE MISSION

Back in 1889, the Rev. Enoch Knock, Minister of the Sandy Lane Methodist Church, called what was to prove to be an eventful meeting in the annals of Methodism in Brown Edge. At that time a rift had arisen between old members - the 'Puritans'- and the young members - the 'Modernists' - and it had come to such a head that Mr Knock decided to intervene.

Led by Mr and Mrs John Charlesworth the Puritans found they could not agree with certain doctrines and modes of worship of the younger set, and had started a series of Sunday morning prayer meetings at Mr Charlesworth's home.

AN ULTIMATUM

From the beginning the Modernists did not approve, and although the Puritans went on paying their stipend to the minister and attended church services regularly, Mr Knock took a serious view of the procedure and gave them a specific time in which to decide whether to discontinue the meetings or to be dismembered from the church.

It was not long after the meeting, well within the time allotted, that the Puritans came to their decision. They broke away from the Sandy Lane Methodist Church and formed a church of their own - The Brown Edge Free Mission.

They first worshipped in the old Primitive Methodist Church, Hill Top, but later Mr Charlesworth bought a timber and corrugated iron mission for £50, and with the help of a local joiner it was erected on Hill Top, near the first mission.

BUILT OWN CHURCH

After a while, however, the structure deteriorated, and when both Mr and Mrs Charlesworth died, it was left to their son, Ralph and his three sons, John, Wilfred and Eber, to build and control a new Mission. Working in their spare time, they and other members constructed the present brick building on the site of the second mission, and are still continuing the work laid down by the first members

Mr Ralph Charlesworth, of Chapel Lane, now in his 82nd year, was its Superintendent until his eldest son John took over about 25 years ago, and his other sons, Wilfred and Eber have been choirmaster and organist respectively for the same period.

The Staffordshire Weekly Sentinel, Friday, July 8th, 1955

Eira Staszko née Mitchell

I was born in 1926 in Norton Green, but a lot of my family live in Brown Edge. My mother was Ellen (Nellie) Dawson and her brother was Tom Dawson's father. I used to visit my grandparents who lived in Heath's Row. Grandfather was Aaron Mitchell and Grandma was Sarah (Sally) Rogers before she was married. I think Grandfather was a miner but he died before the war.

My father was Arthur Mitchell and he had two brothers, Tom and Len, and three sisters - Elsie, Maud and Vera. They lived for a short while at Rose Cottage, opposite the vicarage, then they moved to the middle of Heath's Row. I used to love coming up to Grandma's in the holidays. I remember they had an old tub toilet there, in a brick building outside. We had a flush toilet at home by then. I used to go with Grandad to his allotment that was near the present playing fields, towards Bank End. He kept chickens there as well.

When I was older I went to Brownhills Girls School, but Dad had a bad accident in the mines, and so I left and got a job at Wardle and Davenports in Leek. They called it the Big Mill. When the war came you were not allowed to change jobs so I had to stay until I was about 19.

During the war, when I was about 16, we always came up to Brown Edge on Saturday and Sunday nights. Everybody would be out walking the stretch from the Hollybush to the Roebuck - the 'monkey run' - we'd just walk up and down. In the summer we used to walk from Ball Green down Woodhouse Lane to Knypersley Pool. All the teenagers were there on a Sunday

On Saturday nights we used to love going to the Band Room at Brown Edge. When we used to do what we called the polly glide (palais glide) in a long line, the place would shake. We did the waltz, quickstep and party dances. Sometimes in the interval we'd walk up Hough Hill to the Foaming Quart (later Varsovia Lodge). You could stand in the doorway, as we were underage, and have a shandy. It was very daring and you had to be quick in case somebody saw you and told your dad. The last bus went at 10 o'clock and you had to catch it if you hadn't got anyone to walk you home

After the war, when it came that you could change jobs, I went to work at the pottery firm of Wood & Sons in Burslem. I was working for Charlotte Rhead, the well-known pottery designer, and I was actually the last person that she trained. She lived in Wolstanton and died in 1947 I think. She was a very nice lady and she never married. She'd got a little toy dog and she used to bring it to work with her, carrying it in a scarf. She used to talk very precisely. Her father was Frederick Rhead, also a talented pottery designer, and her mother was French.

It was very interesting work and there were about seven of us in her workshop. I was actually doing tube lining which was drawing the design on wall plaques and fancy ware vases. It was very thin slip that you put in a rubber bag, and you had to squeeze it through a very fine glass tube - very much like doing cake decorating. Charlotte Rhead would always let you add something of your own to the design. Later I went to Moorcrofts in Cobridge doing the same work.

I met my husband, Stefan (Steve) Staszko when he came here after the war. They had weekly dances at Ball Green Club and I met Steve there and he asked me out. He couldn't speak much English. He was working as a miner at Whitfield and living in a miner's hostel in Chell Heath Road where the new doctor's surgery is now. The hostel was just several Nissen huts all joined together, and it was similar to being in the army, with a bunk and a locker. They paid board and had their meals and 'snappin' provided. They had dances there too.

Stefan was born in 1920 in a small village called Macnow in Poland. When he was 19 he was captured by the Russians and arrested for crossing the demarcation line when he was visiting his parents. It was April 1940. He was sentenced to 3 years in a Siberian Labour camp.

After the invasion of Russia by Germany in 1941, the thousands of Polish citizens in the prison camps in Siberia were free to join the Polish army under General Wladyslaw Anders. The release took some time but about 80,000 joined and Stefan was one of these. After a period of convalescence he was given army training and then the regiment was sent to Italy and took part in the attack on Monte Cassino. It was Stefan's first experience of real warfare and he said it was absolute hell.

In July 1946 he arrived in England and went to Thetford in East Anglia, where there was a large Polish Resettlement Camp. After the war 1000s of Polish people were stranded and unable to return to their homeland, without facing the threat of prison for their wartime activities - fighting for their freedom. The Russian government dubbed them 'Anders Men' and many who returned were shot and their families imprisoned.

The men at the camp were offered work in several spheres and Stefan chose coal mining. He chose Stoke-on-Trent because he passed through once on a visit to Blackshaw Moor camp, and found the people very friendly.

Stefan, right, with mining colleagues.

I was 21 when we got married and we lived with my parents at first. After 5 years Stefan was able to apply for and get naturalization. We lived in Burslem for 12 years and later moved to a new house at Brown Edge. The house was built by Harold Bourne. We'd always wanted to live at Brown Edge and we moved in in 1962. We have three children - Linda, Stephanie and Veronica.

We went back to Poland for the first time in 1972 to visit Stefan's mother and family. He never saw his father again, he died in 1951. In May 1984 we joined a group of ex-servicemen and wives to fly to Warsaw to return our army colours to a free Poland.

A few years before Stefan died I managed to get him to talk about his experiences and I wrote down his story. I was pleased to have this published in 2007 for his many friends and family.

Alan Hancock

I was born in 1939 in hospital in Stoke-on-Trent. My father was Joseph Hancock, from Brown Edge and I understand he had been in the army but was on reserve, and was working as a miner. My mother was Kathleen Turnock and her family kept the Swan pub at the bottom of Smallthorne. There were 3 children, my sister Valda and two boys, Ivan and me. Father was called back into service when war came and he served in the North Staffs Regiment. He went with the expeditionary force to France and was killed during the evacuation of

Mum and Dad, Joseph and Kathleen Hancock (née Turnock), c1935.

Dunkirk. There's no known grave and all we've got is a war memorial in Dunkirk

Alan aged 5.

I never remember my mother either, as she died in hospital in 1941. As far as I know there was a family meeting between the Turnocks and the Hancocks as to what to do with us three orphans. My sister Valda went to a branch of the Turnock family in Tunstall, Ivan stopped with Grandma and Grandad Turnock in the Swan, and I came to Brown Edge to my Uncle Billy, my dad's younger brother. Uncle Bill was married to Auntie Florrie who was a Copeland, and she worked at Bullers. She tells me now that one Sunday afternoon Turner's bus came and Grandma Turnock got off, carrying me in her arms, and with my belongings in a carrier bag. Grandma just said *'Here you can have the youngest one.'*

Auntie Flo hadn't got much experience with children but she sent her best friend, Mary Turner, down to Bullers to say that she wouldn't be going any more, as she'd got a child to look after. It was 1941 and there we were - three orphans split up. I think of the three of us I was probably the luckiest one because I came to live at Brown Edge.

Grandma Turnock with Alan, Ivan and Valda, at their mother's grave at Smallthorne Cemetery.

I remember the war years quite well because it was interesting - there were no two roads about it. Where we lived in High Lane, just below The Sytch, you could see the Home Guard practising in the open fields behind us. Mr Taylor, the insurance man who lived round The Sytch, was in the Home Guard and you could see him with his uniform and tin hat on. They'd got guns and everything.

Brown Edge School was interesting. Mrs Powditch, the headmistress, lived just below us down High Lane. She was a lovely woman in many ways but she was a strict disciplinarian. In those days we always wore short trousers, and the form of punishment was across her knee,

LEFT:
Mother, left, with Auntie
Hilda (Dad's sister) 1936.

RIGHT:
Dad, Joseph Hancock,
left, with his brother Bill.

and your trouser leg was yanked up and crack! Mrs Williams was the other teacher because there were only two classes.

I remember there were three of us in the class all with the same birthday - me, Ann Adams and Roy Hargreaves. There were several evacuees in the class as well. I can remember such a lot of the class names - yes it was good. Nobody liked Miss Davenport. Whenever she wore this flowery dress we knew we were in for a bit of a rough day, I don't know what it was.

Uncle Billy and Auntie Flo were strict but very good to me. They later had a daughter, June, and although we were cousins we've always been close and regarded ourselves as brother and sister. One of the benefits of being an orphan was that I was looked after by a lady in Birmingham who came to see me at least once a year. It was like a monitoring process. She always sent me a birthday and Christmas card and I suppose did the same for other war orphans. My fondest memory is of one day, when I was only small, I was told that my brother Ivan and I were going on a trip. I was dressed up that morning in my best coat and a big car pulled up with two ladies wearing air force uniform, and off we went. It was a long journey but I understand that we went to a U.S. army base near to Nottingham. I remember feeling a little bit car sick from time to time - the ladies had us standing by the side of the road

When we got there the Americans were very, very good to us and they showed us all round the workshops and we looked at machine guns and baseball bats. We also saw the aircrafts and tanks. They had huge marquees and even although there was snow on the ground these trestle tables were out and all these soldiers were tucking into the most marvellous food. We had a big dinner and cherry pie and ice cream - it was the first time I'd ever had ice cream.

We were allowed to just walk about the camp and soldiers would lift the tent flaps and say *'Come here son'* and without hesitation they'd make a real fuss of you and they wanted to give you something. I've always thought very kindly of Americans - real genuine people.

I remember it was the first time I'd ever seen a coloured person and it was this huge master

sergeant. He had this British bulldog on a big chain and the dog had the sergeant's stripes tattooed or branded on his side. He said *'Come over here son'* and he gave me chocolates. *'Does your dad smoke?'* When I answered yes he said, *'Take him these'* and gave me a packet of cigarettes. We were the only two boys shown round that day, but when we were driven back the amount of stuff

Alan and Ivan have a memorable day with the Americans c1944. In lower photo, Alan on left and Ivan on right.

we'd been given lasted us weeks and weeks. Every month a parcel used to come with sweets and goodies in that you couldn't get anywhere else. I've always had a soft spot for Americans.

When the village lads were older we went to separate schools but met up again after school at Sandy Lane Methodist Chapel. We went morning, noon and as we got older, at night too, because there was no television in those days. If you went to the pictures on a Sunday you were a sinner and it was a serious offence. Chapel was one of the focal points of village life and it was a good thriving chapel, mainly run by the Weaver family. I remember it with great affection. One of the highlights of my week was after chapel at 3 o'clock, I would walk down the road to Grandma Copeland's where I would collect a homemade cake, a threepenny bit and a comic. She lived at Rock View, opposite Pointon's shop, later Garners.

A main evening activity for young people was sitting and talking on the wall at the Hollybush and then going for walks. Then Arthur Berrisford decided to start a youth club at the chapel and recruited Graham Adderley to help. We used to meet every Friday night in the wooden building and there was always a good turn out.

We would put hardboard shutters to the windows and have a rough game of handball. We had some good trips out to various places. The girls came some nights. There were some nice girls on the village and everyone got on friendly and started courting, in a gentle sort of way I always think.

Village life was always interesting - there was Sammy Bratts, Harrisons and Mrs Johnson's grocery shop and the pubs. There were Turner's buses and Browns and you could set your clock by the buses in those days. We were allowed so much more freedom. I couldn't swim but if the boys were going to Burslem baths you could go - there were no worries about health and safety in those days - you just went

1951 Gymnastic display at
Endon Secondary School,
for the Festival of Britain
Open Day.
L-R:
2nd Alan Hancock, 6th Roy
Dawson, 9th Alan Whieldon.

RIGHT:
A good time at Butlins.
Back: John Sherratt, Malcolm
Chadwick, Ernie Lythcoe.
Seated: Alan, Ken Snape,
Ken Turner, Ron Whitfield,
John Bourne.

Five of the Hancock sisters
L-R: Elsie, Betty, Beryl,
Janet and Annie.

February 1974. Grandad, Frederick William Hancock, celebrating his 90th birthday with his children at the Working Men's Club.

Nearly a hundred walkers set off from the Roebuck public house, Brown Edge, on Sunday morning on a 15-mile walk to Rudyard and back to raise money for charity.

And at the head of the "procession" was 90-years-old Mr. Billy Hancock, one of the village's oldest residents who used to walk to Rudyard 80 years ago.

By the side of Mr. Hancock was the youngest walker, four-years-old Jonathon Hodges of Apple Tree Farm, Sandylane, Brown Edge, who set a fine example to the 90-odd others by completing the whole distance under his own steam.

The organisers of the event led by Mr. and Mrs. John Connell, of the Roebuck, hope to raise £1,000 in all for the Stoke-on-Trent Physically Handicapped Voluntary Aid Group — £600 more than was raised by a similar event last year.

En route and when they got back in Brown Edge, the walkers received free refreshments provided by several food and drink suppliers who "did their bit" towards the day's activities.

Mr. Hancock had his cuppa a little earlier than the rest after calling it a day when he reached the top of Endon Bank. However all the other participants, old and young, completed the distance.

The jaunt was little more than an "appetiser" for voluntary charity worker Mr. Brian Nash, of Shelton, who is planning a 1,000 mile round-Britain walk in the hope of raising about £1,500 for the physically handicapped. Brian is at present busy planning his route and looking for sponsorship from local businessmen.

All who took part had the chance of winning a grocery hamper donated by a well-known firm, the winner being Mrs. Josie White, a barmaid at the Roebuck, who struck on the idea of having a sponsored walk last year.

During the afternoon, everyone retired to a nearby football pitch to see another fundraising event — a match between an Endon schoolboys team and the "Robebuck Regulars," including ex-Port Vale players Tony Toft and Jimmy McClean. The fixture turned out a convincing victory for the Endon lads.

A meal in the TAB, possibly the Over 60s.
Standing: Mrs Dutton, ?, ?, ?, Dorothy Bourne.
Seated: Elsie Lowe, Bill Hancock, Flo Hancock.

Every other Saturday night we used to go as a family to the speedway in Hanley, down Clough Street. They had good crowds there. Turners always ran a bus and the buses were packed at night coming back. It was a good night.

I always remember the film shows in the old workingmen's club. Mr Nixon would come in this old Morris 8 van with 'Nixon's Mobile Cinemas' on the side. I can see him now. People used to come from miles around. The old village members, including my Grandad Hancock, would sit at the back with a pint, by the stove.

Grandad Hancock was a character in his own right and he lived to a good age. He led a walk once from the Roebuck to Rudyard at the age of 90, to raise money for charity. His name was Frederick William and he lived at Bank End. He used to do a lot of poaching and we grew up on rabbit stew.

The Hancock family consisted of 9 children. There was my dad, Joseph, who died, Bill, Arnold and 6 sisters - Elsie, Betty, Hilda, Beryl, Janet and Anne. I remember going to see my Uncle Arnold at home after he'd had a bad accident in the pit and was buried. It was touch and go for him and he was a long time recovering. Then he was struck by lightning when he was fishing and if it hadn't been for his mate, Derek Berrisford, he'd have been a gonner, as he was knocked in the river. Arnold was a real character too.

Uncle Billy (Dad) worked during the war at British Aluminium, but strangely he was pulled from there and had to go to Kemball as a Bevin boy. He worked at Chatterley Whitfield for 3 to 4 years then he went back to British Aluminium at Milton, until it closed. When I was coming up to leaving school he said to me *'Well there's one place you're not going and that's down the pit.'* He was a very gentle man my Uncle Billy.

My ambition though was to be away and off into the forces. One night Graham Adderley gave us a talk on life in the forces. He had done his National Service and served in Germany and Suez. There was a good prospect in those days that the majority of us would have to do National Service. Graham told us about the discipline involved and the places we would visit, and the opportunity to travel. I made up my mind that night that I was going to go.

As I'd lost my dad in the war there was a bit of resistance, to say the least. The family felt that the Hancocks had given enough to the war effort in the First and Second World Wars. I had to compromise, so as I couldn't go in the army I went in the air force. I was only 17 and under strict instructions to sign on for 3 years, which I smiled about as soon as I was on the train at Stoke station. I signed on for 5 years and loved every minute of it.

When I joined the RAF I went down to Cardington for training and became an airframe mechanic. As soon as you take your oath your life changes completely. I later volunteered for 76th squadron, which was operating in the Pacific on Christmas Island, and I worked on the atomic and hydrogen bomb tests. I was based in Australia then Cyprus and later joined the Mountain Rescue Team and went to the Middle East.

I have always been interested in birds since I saw my first dipper at Knypersley and I started rock climbing at an early age, climbing over The Rocks, on my way home from school.

After the RAF I was in Stoke-on-Trent and Staffordshire police for 30 years and then I was an instructor at local outdoor education centres until I was 67. I have had a full life, with a good start and grounding at Brown Edge.

N.STAFFS AIRMAN IN CYPRUS BRAVES CLIFFS FOR BIRDS

A North Staffordshire airman who is a member of the RAF Mountain Rescue Team in Cyprus, is safely back at base after taking part in a successful expedition to ring Eleanora's falcons - one of the rarest birds of prey in the world. He is Senior Aircraftman Alan Hancock of Thelma Avenue, Brown Edge, who is based with the team at RAF Nicosia.

The expedition was arranged at the request of the Cyprus Ornithological Society, whose members are making a special study of these birds which breed in a small colony on the precipitous sea cliffs at Akrotiri, the southernmost point of Cyprus.

The experienced climbers of the rescue team, who have taken part in several dramatic mountain rescues in recent years, went over the cliffs to collect the young birds from their nests. They brought them to the cliff top for ringing by the ornithologists and then went down the cliffs to replace the birds in their nests. Some of the nests were more than 100ft below an overhang, and the climbers had to be lowered down the cliff on two ropes attached to a vehicle on the top of the cliff.

Alan, centre, preparing for his descent.

Radio operators with walkie-talkie sets at the top and bottom of the cliff passed instructions to the men in charge of the ropes who could not see the climbers. A total of 10 young birds from 5 nests were caught by Senior Aircraftman Hancock and his colleagues and it is hoped that as a result more will be learned about migratory movements and possibly their life span.   Sentinel October 16th 1961

Peter Turner

If I had a pound for everybody who said that my grandfather, Sam Turner, had asked their grandfather to go into business with them, I would be quite satisfied. What was true was that they didn't. Sam eventually raised the funds from a loan from The British Wagon Company.

He bought a charabanc with wooden seats and canvas roof that had served in the First World War. He parked it at the bottom of Job's Pool. Just before my Uncle Edwin died a couple of years ago, he told me of the excitement on the village when people saw it on that first morning and how, as a small boy in 1922, he ran down from The Rocks where they lived, to proudly sit inside. It was green and cream, which remained the company colours until the end. The colours were changed for the 'deckers' in the early 60s to Tudor maroon, as this was easier to keep clean.

Grandfather was born in 1883, in Sandy Lane. His parents were Samuel and Mary Anne Turner. His mother's maiden name was Twigge and she came from North Wales. My great grandfather, also Samuel Turner, was born at Brown Edge too, in 1858.

To pay for the bus Sam changed his job from working at Whitfield to welding chains at the Chain Works at Ford Green, where the pay was more and his shifts were different, which enabled him to run the buses. Sam was descended from a long line of master blacksmiths from Longsdon so I suppose this also appealed, as perhaps did the allocation of two quarts of ale per day, brought over to the welders from the Ford public house. Good job they didn't have breathalysers then!

The early days saw him fetching and carrying miners from Whitfield to Brown Edge, which the company continued to do for the next 70 years. Two nice stories that I have been told relate to the relationship he had with the colliers. One told me that Sam always gave them a fag when they got on the bus (miners couldn't carry 'contraband' cigarettes and matches on their person). This clearly was a good way to build business.

Frankie Holdcroft told me that amongst others he used to act as conductor and collect money. One day he found a five pound note tucked in the moneybag and told Sam. Sam said it had been there for a while and he was waiting to see who would tell him first, and did he want a job!

Whitfield pit has many memories for me personally, because as soon as I could walk until I went to school, my Uncle Edwin used to take me on the bus at dinner time to drop off the miners on noons and to pick up the men on days. This is how I learned to drive as the conductor would stand me on the front seat, with the little window open, and Uncle Edwin would say *'Listen to the engine and tell me when to change gear'*. I don't know what the miners thought as we lurched up Duke Bank.

I also had memories of sitting on the knee of the driver of the cage of the Hesketh Pit and seeing the cable run out from this great engine. I wasn't sure about this as it surely was dangerous, but I was telling this to John Chadwick and he said it was true, as it was him who operated the cage. He of course lived opposite the garage that Grandad built in 1926 in High Lane. This wasn't our first garage, as he used to park where Cross Edge Road is now (also where the Post Office is now). I don't know which garage it was, but as it was made of oil drums and planks, it was blown away in a gale!

Sam was supported in his business venture by his wife, Harriet Tomkinson, the daughter of Daniel (Tunny) Tomkinson. They were married in 1909. She was the cousin of Mrs Sam Bratt, Mrs Basnett and Mrs Berrisford and Lottie Hayes, which just typifies the Brown Edge community.

A 1947 AEC Regent III outside Turner's Garage. This ex-London Transport bus was bought by Turners in 1958, and had a Weymann body.   *Courtesy of J Basnett.*

Shortly after the charabanc, Sam bought another bus and retired the old one (it was a hencote in the back garden when I was a boy.) This new bus was soon added to when he bought Lee Burgess's business from him. Grandad then left the Chain Works and started running a public service vehicle to Burslem (which changed to Hanley shortly after) and taking the mill girls to Leek, which again conveniently had different shifts than the miners.

The trip to Leek wasn't easy. Uncle Gordon once told me that people were frightened when the bus used to go 'round the corkscrew' and that some caught the train to Endon and then caught the bus up to Brown Edge. It was quite a while before I realised that the corkscrew was the name of the road before the new cutting was made at Longsdon.

I have a photograph of Uncle Gordon as a young man at Ilam, in front of two buses, on a Sunday mystery trip. He said that was the first time a bus had been down there, and to get back all the passengers had to get out and push the bus up Blore pastures, because it was too steep.

A 1961 Bedford coach bought new by Turners in 1961. It had a Plaxton body.   *Courtesy of J Basnett.*

He had lots of stories like that. He used to love driving; he hardly ever looked at the road just looking round at the scenery and talking to passengers! On one Llandudno trip he went off to Conway and tried to get across the bridge there, only to find out that it was too sharp a bend at the end to cross. A helpful local told him that no bus had ever crossed the bridge, and he would have to wait until they built the proposed new bridge! So Uncle Gordon got out of the bus, had a good look, reversed back, turned round and reversed over the bridge and managed to turn the corner, much to the dismay of the locals.

Harriet died in 1954 and Sam died shortly afterward and on his death certificate the official cause of death is 'died of a broken heart'.

I could say so much more about the business I was born in to and loved. The memories of incidents that happened keep flooding back, the local dialect that was used, as well as the knowledge and wisdom that was passed from Sam to his four sons - Gordon, Edwin, Alan, Roy (my father) and his daughter, Olwyn, all of whom have passed away now.

I still get people calling at 'The Garage' or dropping notes in telling me of what is happening to the buses. One is supposedly in USA, painted red, another was in Germany but has been brought back to the Potteries, where it is going to be restored and painted up in our colours. Another is in a yard on the Wirral, which again is supposedly going to be restored, so perhaps my final journey will indeed be possibly like my first - back from Leek hospital on one of Sammys.

George Mayer and his buses - John Basnett

In 1923 George Mayer of Hill Top purchased a small coach and sucessfully operated a service from Lask Edge. This went via Brown Edge to Burslem on Saturdays, and from Lask Edge to Leek on Wednesdays. He also took miners to Norton and Mill girls to Leek. He later operated two buses which he kept in a garage behind Harvey's Mission at Hill Top.

He sold his small business in 1932 to Browns Motor Company of Tunstall, and he became one of their drivers.

George with wife Alice.

George Mayer's bus at Hill Top, a 1930 Dennis. The Colliers Arms is in the background.

Florence Adderley née Simcock

I was born in 1934 at Job's Pool at my grandparent's home - it's called The Villas. My father's name was Joseph William Simcock and my mother was Sarah Ann Bailey, before she was married. They had 13 children and I was the 8th one. There was Jack, Joan, Howard and Enoch, Joseph, Violet, Nancy, myself, Brian, Frank, Raymond, Keith and David. Howard and Enoch died - one at 2 years and one at 10 months.

Five of Flo's brothers. Back: Brian, Frank and Raymond. Front: Keith and David.

I was the last one to be born at The Villas, as when I was 3 months old we moved to a cottage at the top of Fiddler's Bank - the end one of three. My brother Brian lives there now - everybody knows Brian. It's been altered a lot. We rented the cottage, all three were owned by Turners. Mabel and Jack Turner lived in the middle one and Nicholls in the other end one. I remember Nicholls came when Michael was a baby in a pram. Our cottage had three bedrooms but the larger one had a partition with girls one side and boys the other. At one stage we slept five in a bed.

Yes we grew up on Fiddlers and played up there. You had to have one leg longer than the other to stand level up there. We used to have a right good team for rounders. When Mrs Shallcross was looking after her parents I used to take her daughter Irene out and do shopping for her. I used to have Irene and our David in the pushchair, and shopping, and push all the way up there. By the time you'd finished carrying shopping up there you had arms like a monkey.

We had to fetch water from a well down the backfield or from the one below the Foaming Quart - we had to fetch 25 buckets on washday. We had no electric on - it was just oil lamps.

Flo's mum Sarah Ann Simcock (née Bailey) delivering the post.

Mother always had to go out to work. She delivered post in the country area, walking as far as Lask Edge Chapel and the Tower at Knypersley. I was only about 9 but had to look after the five lads who were all young. I used to night feed our David, the youngest. We made all the children's clothes. Mum kept us all healthy with cod liver oil - she used to just say, *'Hold your nose.'* We all had to line up for our brimstone and treacle too.

We always kept animals - ducks, geese, hens and a pig and we had a big vegetable garden. We grew a whole field of potatoes. It all helped.

Dad worked at Chatterley Whitfield and walked through the fields. He lived to be 77 but a lot of them died in pit accidents. Grandfather, Enoch Simcock, who lived at Job's Pool, was a pitman as well. Great Uncle Fred lived in a little cottage opposite where Underwoods live - it used to be old Eli Heath's place.

I remember water being there at Job's Pool. My brother nearly got drowned on the tail end of the pool there. I remember them filling the pool in, by the house. There was a big lake all down the valley and there used to be a big pool up The Vale where Pointons lived. There used to be water round the old school and New Lane. We used to take our shoes off and paddle across it, going home from school. The houses in Sandy Lane are on a peat bog.

Sandy Lane. Flo was born in the house on the right.

I'm sure it's my Uncle Fred on the front of the book *A Brown Edge History* as he always wore a dickey bow and is outside The Villas. Dad was the rough and ready man and Uncle Fred the dandy man. I think my dad's on as well and some of the older children. Grandad bred canaries and budgies in that shed in the picture, at the right of the house - it was lovely in that shed.

My Grandma Simcock was in Buffalo Bill's 'Wild West Show' - she was a dancer. Her dance name was Lizzie Wilson but her real name was Catherine Hickey.

We were always told that Great Grandma Simcock eloped from Kilkenny Castle in Ireland when she was 16, with her childhood sweetheart. Her father was an army man and they lived in the castle. Her soldier sweetheart joined the Stafford's Regiment He was a deserter from the Irish army for one week, but they let him in. It's always been talked about in the family.

When we were children we saw the plane crash over Broad Lane. We were picnicking over the other side of the wall near the shed up there. We were watching it come over, on fire, and we saw me father coming like hell to fetch us. There'd have been six out of one family gone if we'd been in the wrong place. There was John Harvey, Tom Nicholls, June Hewitt, and our family - Pete, Raymond, Frank, Brian, Nancy and me.

When we saw this plane and all this black smoke belching out of the back we couldn't shove our sandwiches in the case quick enough. Mother used to give us a case with food in and some wartime orange juice - we had it for years after rationing. The ground shook and it was very noisy. We were very lucky; I don't know how it didn't hit the hut. We just saw two men and a woman get out. The woman got out, combed her hair and wanted a fag, and then she saw all us kids and told us to get down in a ditch somewhere, as the tanks might blow.

Weeks later we watched them cart the plane away and we collected bits of the thick glass that were lying everywhere. We made rings and crosses and all sorts of things with the bits

We were very poor but everybody was poor then. I think people were kinder with each other - you helped each other. Some people used to have pigs, and have them slaughtered, and be sharing the food out. My father and old man Hancock poached everything they could lay their hands on, but they shared it all out. Lottie Hayes used to keep the Roebuck and we used to have to deliver rabbits there, to the back door - big ones were 1 shilling and small ones 9d.

Some of my brothers went into mining and some went into farming - you just did what you were told. I got told I'd got to go in the mills, for the money, to help keep the five lads. I worked for Job Whites at Compton Mill, in Leek, which is now an antiques place.

My grandad told us a story once, that there was a man found hanging in the trees at the top of the playing field footpath, as it comes on to what is now Thelma Avenue. They never found anybody for it. Grandad used to be a gravedigger but he was cremated - he didn't want the worms to eat him! My Great Grandma, Mary Simcock, was a village midwife.

I met my husband, Graham Adderley, when he was on leave from the army. He did two and a half years National Service then three years as a reserve. He was in one of the first units that went into Suez. He didn't have his medal until he died.

We were married in 1955 at Sandy Lane Chapel and had a reception at the Band Room. We moved in with Graham's parents in Thelma Avenue and as they were not well we nursed them both. I have lived there ever since.

Flo and Graham Adderley 1955.

My mother used to tell us lots of old riddles that had been passed on and I still remember some of them - here they are:

Purple, yellow, red and green	Tobacco is a sinful weed	Around around a rick
The king can't reach it	And from the devil doth proceed	Come across me Uncle Dick
Nor can the Queen	Burns your pockets	Pulled off his head
Nor can the Lord Mayor	Scents your clothes	Drank his blood
Whose power's so great	And makes a chimney of	Left his body standing
Tell me this riddle	your nose.	
While I count to eight		(Answer - a bottle of beer)

(Answer - a rainbow)

Ken Turner - Sandy lane Methodist Chapel

I was born in 1937 in the cottage in Sandy Lane now known as Banbury Cottage. My parents were Iris and Harry Turner. My mother's maiden name was Langford and she originated from Smallthorne. I have one brother, Philip. When I was about three we went to live with my granddad, Thomas Turner, who was a coal dealer. He lived at Leak's Cottage on the corner of Sandy Lane and Thelma Avenue. My grandma died before I was born. She was Charlotte Elizabeth Sheldon.

When my Grandad remarried we went to live in High Lane, below The Sytch. Alan Taylor lived opposite and Alan Hancock lived next door. The three of us spent a lot of time together over the next fifteen years or so.

My father worked for my Grandad while he had the coal business. When my grandad sold the business and retired my father went back to working in the pits (he had worked at Black Bull - Victoria Colliery in his early years). He worked in the pits until he retired. He died in 1976.

I went to Sandy Lane Methodist Sunday School up to the age of about eight or nine. I then transferred my affections to St Anne's Church Sunday School where I stayed until I was about 16, when I began to go to Sandy Lane Methodist Youth Club, which was started and run by Arthur Berrisford. Through this attachment I began to get involved with the Church, an association I have maintained ever since. My wife, Pauline, was a Weaver and her family had a longstanding attachment to Sandy Lane.

There has been a Wesleyan Society in Sandy Lane for over 200 years. It was founded in about 1798. The members listed were: Ralph Wood, William Tomkinson, Martha Willott, Judy Mountford, Joseph and James Willott, Joseph and William Mountford, Mary and William Fox, another Mary Fox, Hugh and Margaret Willott, Joseph Bailey and Henry Warner.

There is an account by Hugh Bourne, still then a Wesleyan, that on *'Tuesday March 1st 1803 - a very wet day, I had by desire to go to Brown Edge at night, which was rather a cross it being rainy... when I came there I had the happyness of seeing a larger congregation than usual'*. He doesn't record how many attended but it sounds as if there were more than currently attend our regular Sunday services (perhaps with the exception of the first Sunday family services).

It seems that at that time there was no chapel building - the meetings being held at John Sargent's house in Woodhouse Lane. The first chapel building was registered in 1805 and it consisted of a single room with a large pot stove in the middle. It was situated in Sandy Lane opposite the existing building. This first chapel was sold in 1962 to Mrs Docksey and was a clothes shop for a while, but is now a domestic garage.

James Simcock built the new chapel and there was a stone laying ceremony on May 30th 1901, recorded in the Burslem Circuit Magazine;

'May 30th was a Fete day at Sandy Lane. At 2.30 people began to arrive on foot, by trap, by broke and by 3.00pm the road was full of friends. Mr Withington briefly spoke, and then called on Rev. E Thompson, Chairman of the district, for his address. Foundation stones were laid by Mr C D Heaton, Mr R Heath, Mr S Lawton, Mr T Arrowsmith, Mr Goodwin, Mr Bratt and Mr J Gardiner. Tea was provided in a large tent behind the new chapel.'

The new chapel was opened on the 5th November that year. The Sunday school was well attended - there were nearly a hundred children and it took place in a wooden hut. When I went to the Sunday school Pauline's grandfather, Charlie Weaver, was the Superintendent and he was a real character. He left the chapel and went to the Free Mission for a while. I think he'd

A rear view of the old wooden Sunday School building.

The interior of the old Sunday School 1961.There was a pot stove at either end and a harmonium.

BELOW:
Members of the Sunday School.

had a bit of a fall-out, but he came back when the mission closed. Arthur and Freda Berrisford were two of the Sunday school teachers. Later Arthur Berrisford started a youth club, which was very popular.

EXTRACTS FROM THE METHODIST QUARTERLY NEWSLETTER.

1962 - an evening trip to Cheadle and Ashbourne. At the Sunday School Anniversary service there were congregations of well over 200.

1963 - an outing to Southport - Sunday school treat.

1963 - youth club - average 40 members - ladies in short supply. Activities at present - weight training, table tennis, courses in art and judo. Agenda for coming months - 15th March - film show. 22nd March - a party going to The Victoria Theatre, Hartshill

Social committee: musical entertainment and a conjuring performance. Annual Christmas party. 26th January A pantomime, Jack and the Beanstalk was presented by Mr and Mrs Turner and it included some Sunday school scholars and members of the junior club. A concert by Biddulph Moor Prize Band.

Early in 1961 the Church embarked on a scheme of planned giving, whereby everyone who had any connection with the Church was approached and asked to pledge a regular amount of giving. In return the Church undertook not to approach them for any donations to Church funds. The aim of this was that the Church would have a firm idea what its future income would be and to help pay off the outstanding debt on the new school hall, which had already been commissioned. A target of £3000 in promises was set and this was achieved. In fact a total of £3300 was actually received over the next three years.

The new hall was built (by Cousens and Allport of Burslem) for the sum of £8794 14s 2d and officially opened in September 1961 by Charles Weaver. The inaugural address was given by Rev. Fred Bourne who was himself a Brown Edger and who had been attached to the Church in earlier years.

Members in the old chapel. This lovely building built in 1901 was sold in 1980, later demolished and new property built on the site.

Grandad Thomas Turner in front of Leak's Cottage.

The cottage in Sandy Lane c1937 where Ken was born. His mother Iris Turner (née Langford) is at the gate.

LEFT: Sandy Lane Chapel Garden Party late 1950s. Music provided by the Lion's Paw Ramblers, later to become Bri Martin and the Marauders.
L-R: Keith Fisher, ?, Brian Oakes, ?.

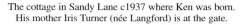

BELOW:
Members of Sandy Lane Chapel 1957.
Standing: Alan Hancock, Brian Williams, Malcolm Chadwick, Ken Turner, Kenneth Snape, Pauline Weaver, June Bourne, Ernie Lythcoe, Sylvia Shaw, Hilary Walker, Duncan Hall, Derek Berrisford, Jill Swarbrook, Richard Davis, John Sherratt, John Bourne, ?, Valerie Bettany, Mrs Myatt, ?.
Seated: Mavis Harrison, ?, Christine Wilcox, Beatrice Nash, Mr W G Myatt, Miss M Monks, Rev.Wilfred Harper, Rev.Attoe, Arthur Berrisford, Enoch Goodwin, ?.

The existing Chapel building was closed in 1980 due to the cost of maintenance having to be borne by a dwindling membership. The last wedding to take place there was that of Sheila Slater and Clive Proctor on 15th June 1975.

The membership of the church is now eight, which is about the average attendance at 'normal' Sunday services; the attendance at the 'First Sunday' family services is about twice that figure.

Young peoples' work in the form of the weeknight 'J Gang' is led by John Claydon ably assisted by Rita Elden. He also leads a week-long children's mission in the summer school holidays.

Building of the new Sunday school in progress 1961.

SANDY LANE METHODIST CHURCH
BROWN EDGE

✠

UNITED SUNDAY SCHOOL RALLY

TO CELEBRATE THE OPENING
OF THE NEW SCHOOL HALL

SUNDAY, 22nd OCTOBER, 1961

at 2-30 p.m.

✠

Chairman : MR. C. POWELL
Speaker : MR. K. MORRIS
Soloist : MRS. S. QUAYLE

The laying of the foundation stone for the new Sunday school 1961. L-R: Albert Mountford, ?, Enoch Goodwin, Rev. Atkinson, Herbert Bourne, Rev. A G Utton.

The official opening of the Sunday School October 1961. L-R: Rev.Norman Hallam, Rev.Kenneth Armitstead, Rev. K Atkinson, Herbert Bourne, Rev.Peter Hanks, Rev.Fred Bourne, Enoch Goodwin, Charles Weaver, Rev. AG Utton.

Eric Slack

I was born in 1926 at The Rocks. My parents were Annie and Samuel Heath Slack. Mother's maiden name was Baddeley, and her mother was Harriet Baddeley who kept the little shop where Keith's

Eric's Grandma, Harriet Baddeley, outside her shop.

supermarket is now. Mum had a brother Arthur - just the two of them.

I had two brothers, George and Sam and a sister, Grace. I was at Granny's shop all the time when I was a little 'un. Every Sunday Granny used to have one of us for Sunday dinner and me and my brother George used to fall out as to whose turn it was to go. She had the shop for a long time and I've always known it. She sold general groceries, sticks, and sweets - anything really. She was a very nice lady. I remember she used to make her own treacle toffee and sell it in the shop. She had lots of jars of sweets from the agent as well. I used to laugh when she had an order of cigarettes from the wholesalers. We used to collect cigarette cards that were in the packets and keep them in an album. George and me used to go through all the packs and change them with ours that we'd got too many of. The deliveries came by horse and cart then.

On the left side of the shop there used to be a chicken run. A little building on the right was a little wash place and next to that was a building that is still standing today - Brian's hairdressers. The shop went back quite a bit and there was a little toilet outside at the back.

Granny wanted to give me piano lessons and she said if I got some books she'd teach me, but I never did. We used to love playing dominoes with Grandma and

Mum and Dad, Samuel Heath and Annie Slack (née Baddeley).

Grandad, but they always used to fall out and say one of them was cheating. I've still got the domino set now.

Grandad always came with his shotgun - he used to go poaching up Tinster's Wood. When Grandma died in 1945 Keith Berrisford's mother bought the shop, they were at the Lump of Coal then. Grandad, George Baddeley, came to live with us at 130 High Lane. He died in April 1967 aged 95.

I always used to hang around Bratt's butchers and slaughterhouse and watch 'em killing. A chap called Bourne used to slaughter for him. They had to get the beef by road then, there were no cattle wagons. Mr Bratt used to say *'come Newcastle with us.'* We walked all the way to Newcastle, then

Grandad George Baddeley in High Lane, c1962.

Eric's wife Beryl Hancock as the Victory Queen in 1946. Marie Turner is on her right.

back with the cows - you used to think nothing of it then.

When I left school I went to work on stockings at Wardle and Davenports at Leek, then went to Swynnerton during the war, making shells. In the meantime I had a letter saying I'd got to go as a Bevin Boy, in the pit. I said to my dad *'I'm not going down the pit, there's three of you down there already.'* *'Please yourself '* he said. So what I did, without his knowledge, I went and joined up. I signed for the navy on June 19th 1943 when I was exactly 17 and a half, as you couldn't join until then. The place for signing on was at Bethesda Street in Hanley.

I had 6 weeks training at Plymouth on HMS Rally then went to Portsmouth and on to the Orkney Islands. I worked on convoy ships in the North Atlantic, keeping guard over supply ships - all different carriers and cruisers. There'd usually be about 20 ships in a convoy.

There were about 200 men on board. Officers had their own rooms but we all slept in hammocks slung up over the dining tables and do you know they were lovely and comfortable. In the morning they used to say *'Shift out of the way, we want to get breakfast.'*

You got scared. The convoy was always being attacked and torpedoes were worse. I had a narrow escape once when we were near Russia. A submarine was attacking our ships, and one or two went down. I was observing it from the bridge with my binoculars. It was pretty scary, but I landed safely back in Scapa Flow in the Orkneys. All the ships came into Scapa, as that was the main base. I was in Ireland at the end of the war, on HMS Trouncer.

I scraped through it. I did 4 years and wished I'd stopped on, in later life. I still remember my number - P/JX570085. All my navy mates have nearly gone - Billy Dale and Stan Snape. There's only Fred Rolinson left. Fred's wife, Nora, taught me how to dance at Ball Green Club.

After the war I went to work at British Aluminium at Milton and when it closed, Joshua Wardles at Leekbrook - it's houses now. My dad was killed at Chatterley Whitfield. He was coupling a wagon up and one came down on him and hit his head. He was 52.

I met my wife, Beryl Hancock, at the Brown Edge carnival where she had a stall selling ice cream. I bought one and that was that. We were married for 57 years.

Eric and Beryl's wedding. Back: Betty Clowes, Billy Dale, Hilda Docksey, Fred. William Hancock, Grace Beardmore, Joan Slack, Sam Slack.
Front: Clifford Docksey, Gladys Taylor, Annie Slack, Eric and Beryl, Amy Hancock, William Hancock, Janet Hancock, Arnold Hancock, Josephine Clowes, Annie Morris, Philip Docksey.

Merle Whitehall née Tyler

I was born in 1936 in Robert Heath Street, Smallthorne. My parents were John James Tyler and Doris, whose maiden name was Birch. Dad was an overman at Chatterley Whitfield. Bill Grindy was building some new houses at Brown Edge and my parents saved a deposit of £100. When they asked Mr Grindy he said it was enough deposit for 2 houses, so they bought 2 and rented one out. The road was Thelma Avenue, named after Mr Grindy's daughter, Thelma - now Thelma Steele. I was about 11-13 months old when we came to live there.

Mum and Dad had 7 children - Roy, Stan, Doris, me, James, Susan and Leonard. James died. Dad was always busy. He mended shoes and was always making toys and things. He made toys for children in the avenue - cradles and little barrows, leather purses etc.

I started school at the infant's when I was 4, so that makes it 1940. I remember eating the harvest - apples, carrots and turnips etc - they were all washed and cut up in small pieces and you helped yourself. It was a real treat. Mrs Powditch was the headmistress and she introduced me to the world of imagination. There were few books available then, and she would lend me books from her own collection. I would go to her house in High Lane and the book would be wrapped in a teacloth. *'Keep them clean and wash your hands before you start reading,'* she would say.

I remember going into the air raid shelter when the siren went at Norton and sometimes we would have a practice. The little lads would drag the milk crates in and we'd have our own little bottles. We were with Mrs Powditch and Mrs Williams and were singing songs and nursery rhymes. We always had to carry our little boxes with the gas masks in.

We had gift boxes from America - tins with a gift in and sweets and chewing gum. We went up in alphabetical order to the front of the class. I remember Thelma Grindy going up and Mrs Powditch was going to give her this box and then changed her mind and got another one. Doreen Finney had the first one and the gift was a silver cross and chain. It always stuck in Thelma's memory, as her gift was mediocre.

When I was in the infant's we got snowed in one day. Parents dug us out with spades and the drift was 4 foot deep from the window to the front wall. As we walked down St Anne's Vale the snow was up to our knees, over our wellies. We thought it was absolutely wonderful. They didn't close the school! They fetched bread from Smallthorne on sledges.

Mrs Baddeley's shop was where Keiths is now. You went down about three steps to it and we used to go for liquorice and kali. There was linoleum on the counter and there was always a little toffee hammer there.

My parents used to take hot coals off the fire to take upstairs into the small tiled fireplace in our bedroom. There was no central heating in those days, in the 1940s. Ice would make patterns on the window until you were not able to see through them. The nice bit on a winter's night would be to take up the oven shelf, wrapped up in a towel. It was moved around in the bed to warm it and then left at the bottom, to put your feet on. Another memory of my childhood was syrup of figs - every child had to have a daily dose!

We moved to Sandy Lane and my mother had a grocery and hardware store. We swapped houses with Gordon and Rose Turner. We opened about 8 o'clock and it was not uncommon for someone to come to the back door after we had closed, to buy something they had forgotten. If we were eating our tea the family would put their hands over their plates, because the family joke was that Mother would sell the cakes off the table.

One night, coming up to 10 o'clock, we had a knock at the door. Mum had gone round the

Roebuck for a couple of Guinness and we had to stay in with the younger ones. It was Harry Frost from the top pub. He said, *'Give us a couple of dummies'* and we asked him *'what colour?'* He said *'Never mind what colour.'* We came out with the card of dummies and asked him which he wanted. He said, *'How many is there on that card - we'll have all that - we'll have one for every bloody room!'* The baby was Dudley.

Everything was on ration and you had to have coupons for tea, sugar, sweets, cheese and fats etc. If I remember rightly it was $1^1/_2$oz of cheese, 1oz of tea and 2oz of fat - I wonder how we would go on today? (We should be a bit slimmer!)

Dad had a little printing press and used to print tickets for dances and concerts. Mother was a bit of an agony aunt. The ladies would come into the shop and tell her their problems as they sat on the potato sack on the other side of the counter. I often think of those times spent behind a shop counter, serving customers with their weekly shop (it would all fit into one shopping basket) especially as I look into the shopping trolleys at supermarkets today. The small shop was an important part of village life - a hub of the community. Its demise marked the end of an era.

We had such fun growing up on the village with the chapel, Nixon's mobile cinema and the Band Room. In the evening my friend Lorna Durber and I used to dash home for a quarter to 7 to listen to Dick Barton - special agent on the radio. There was also Paul Temple and we also

Silver Wedding of Doris and John James Tyler (Merle's mum and dad) in the old Working Men's Club late 1940s.

liked Donald Peers on a Sunday afternoon - 'By a babbling brook' - we used to sing it. At home we were always singing and playing the piano.

Although time has changed our thinking and day-to-day living, I think every belief and most opinions we hold go back to the childhood we spent on Brown Edge. Nothing is as lasting in our minds as the lessons we were taught in our childhood.

Queen Ann Egan with her retinue 1966.
L-R: Louise Harvey (Merle's daughter), ?Jones, Kevin Snape, Helen Bourne, Alison Mosedale, Ann Egan, ? Jones, ?, Jackie Snape, ?.

Greenway Bank and the Heath family - Robert Bailey

As our farm was right next to the Hall where the Heaths lived we were always closely connected. They were Robert William Heath, known locally as Billy, his wife Phyllis, and their two sons, Robert Edward, and John. As the latter two were about the same age as my parents they always referred to them as Johnny and Master Bobby.

Greenway Bank, 1970.
It is reputed to have been bought by Hugh Henshall Williamson in about 1778, and was later acquired by the Heath family.
It was bought by Staffs.CC. in 1972 and demolished, after being vandalised.

We delivered milk to the hall twice a day. As a child, I can remember going to the huge back door and pulling the bell. Mrs Boyd was the cook then. I remember Mrs Phyllis coming to pay the milk bill. She always used a fountain pen to write the cheque and always blotted it. We children had to be quiet up the corner. I think Mr Robert, the son, lived in London then, because he was an underwriter for Lloyds. He had had polio as a child and was partially crippled. He never married. He used to drive a Lanchester, a green convertible.

Mr Robert Edward Heath in his library.
He was the last person to reside at the Hall.

Mr Robert's brother Johnny used to visit, and he had his own private aircraft. He'd circle round a couple of times and then the butler would shoot off to collect him from the aerodrome - Meir I think. He'd always come and visit Grandad and Uncle James and stand talking in the cowshed at milking time. One of my vivid memories of him was his highly polished brown boots. He actually farmed at Knypersley End Farm for a while. When he married he went to Sussex and farmed a large estate there. He died in 1965.

Mr Robert was friends with Colonel Leese from The Moor House, Biddulph Park. You'd quite often see them driving out together.

When you stood in Greenway Bank Hall and you looked out through the windows, you could never see the industry which the Heath family had created. Trees were always planted strategically to hide any of the works. There were no fence lines in the fields that surrounded it, thus giving the impression of rolling countryside.

We used to go into the kitchen when we delivered the evening milk to the Hall and Mrs Boyd would be preparing dinner. She used to let us grind the coffee - it became one of our little chores. She'd always got a toffee jar on the top shelf. After the war there were no sweets about so you'd eye this jar up and she'd always give you one. One night she let me have some toast with kidney on. I had never had it before - ooh it was lovely - something I've never forgotten. One Christmas time I remember Mrs Heath bringing us crystallised ginger - that was something else we didn't normally have.

Keeper's Cottage, 1966. Fred Chaddock is standing on the ladder.

Mrs Boyd used to live in and used to go back to her family three weeks at a time. This was when Mr and Mrs Turner, from Biddulph, came to stay to do the cooking. She had been the cook before Mrs Boyd. It always appeared that when Mrs Turner was there the Heaths did more entertaining. I think she was better at it. This was when they had parties coming to play croquet. Quite often on a summers evening, we children were told to keep quiet because there were guests round the croquet lawn which adjoined the farmyard. This was in the early 50s. William Heath died 1st April 1954 and then I remember Phyllis died 10th October 1955.

My sister, Hilda, lives in Keeper's Cottage with her husband David Sheldon. It was originally owned by the estate and was where the gamekeeper lived. There has been no gamekeeper there in my lifetime. I first remember two families living there. They were Len and Gertie Green and Mr and Mrs Rogers, along with their two children, Kenneth and Eric. In the early 50s Len Green used to sell fishing tickets for Knypersley Pool. When they left, Fred Chaddock, who worked at our farm, and his wife Ivy, came to live there. Ivy worked at the Hall. They had two children and Ivy's grandparents, the Farells, were living there as well.

There was a shooting incident once - it was before I was born. It was the poachers versus the keepers. The police were not far away. Grandfather was with the keepers and one of them was shot in the leg. He was not seriously injured because he'd got thick leather leggings on. Unfortunately, when he was shot, I've been told he issued the instruction 'shoot to kill'. This never came out in court. Shortly after the incident the keepers were 'quietly' disbanded. There was never any pheasant shooting after.

The Heaths had their own private laundry, the house at the end of the farm drive. It is called Bank Top House now, but to us it's still the 'laundry'. In one of the rooms there was no ceiling; it went right up to the roof of the house. There were racks on pulleys used for drying the washing. The other room, adjacent to it, had a wooden stillage round two walls as if that was for ironing on and laying out the laundry.

A present day photo of the Laundry, now a private residence.

On the east side there was a kitchen and a room with a bay window, which was the living accommodation. The last butler to live at the laundry was Joe Maddock and his family.

Up until the estate being sold in May 1972, the Serpentine Pool was private. It wasn't officially open to the public - it was always out of bounds, even to us. There used to be a huge oak door round by the fisheries, as you start across the path, which was always locked. Having gone through it and following the leat alongside of Knypersley Pool, you came to a little stone bridge. The bridge led to the wishing well which was set in a wall within an arched tunnel. You went up some steps and the well was on the right. It's all collapsed in now. It was more or less opposite the boathouse. There were two boathouses, one on the Pool and one on the Serpentine.

Across the dam, between the two pools, there were rhododendron hedges on either side of the path. Mr Robert used to keep them trimmed even though he was on two sticks. I remember several occasions when I was quite small seeing him working, clearing the ditches out and trimming the hedges. Two chaps from Bemersley, Mo Booth and Sam Heath helped him.

The gardens were always kept lovely at the Hall. There used to be two gardeners. The head

Gardener's House early 1970s.

The Rose Gardens.

gardener lived at Gardeners House, which is down the farm drive. My brother-in-law, Robert Holdcroft lives there now with his wife Julie. There was a lovely rose garden to the north of the Hall, with the croquet lawn on the east of it and the vegetable gardens were between the Hall and the farm drive, which is currently used as a car park for the Country Park.

Some of the gardeners and their families I remember were Mr Bunce, Mr Middleton, Mr Preston, Mr Sturgess, Mr Jones and Mr Reg Pope. Mr Pope was the last resident gardener, and from then on George Bailey looked after the gardens in his spare time. He worked on the buses and didn't live here. It was amazing how tidy he kept everywhere. He and his wife went on to run the flower shop in Biddulph.

All the greenhouses were used when I was small - there were vines and tomatoes etc. I was more interested when they were fumigating them - being interested in matches! There was always a lot of smoke about. They were in the vicinity of where the top car park is now. They were heated by a big boiler, which was by the Gardener's House. It had a tall chimney. They had loads of coal or coke, whatever, tipped on the

Gardener's Cottage c1959. Joe and Hannah Wood outside.

farm drive. Going back, Heath's owned all the pits, so they had their own fuel supply.

The under-gardener's house was called Gardener's Cottage. It's been taken down now. The last people to live there were Joe and Hannah Wood. Mr Wood farmed at Willfield Lane Brown Edge and when he retired they came to the cottage. He also did jobs for Mr Heath.

A family named Hollinshead lived in the cottage at one time. He wasn't a gardener. He used to park his car round in the courtyard at the Hall. He said to Mr Heath *'Don't be surprised if you hear me going out during the night, sometimes I work nights'.* One Saturday, we were returning from the milk round and there were several official looking men, wearing trilbies and long raincoats, en route. I was about nine at the time. They were waiting for Mr Hollinshead to come in. He was suspected of stealing a safe from one of the builders, in the Stoke area. Later in the evening, when he returned home, he must have realised the detectives were waiting for him and so he threw a bundle of notes behind the dustbin. The next morning the money was blowing all across the farm drive. Me and my sister Elizabeth saw it - 10/- notes and £1 notes floating about. We ran back and told Mother and she rang the police. They came and searched and found a lot of the money hidden in a doll's pram. Mr Hollinshead was convicted and sent to prison. Someone who lived at the Warder's Tower was involved too.

The last of the Heaths to live at the Hall, Mr Robert Edward Heath, is buried at Brown Edge Church in an unmarked grave. The Heaths, as the Williamsons before them, were great benefactors to Brown Edge. I believe the vicar of Brown Edge came to see Mr Heath for afternoon tea, and as they walked up the Rose Gardens, he pointed through the trees to Brown Edge Church, to the spot where he wanted to be buried.

Mr Robert left Greenway Bank after a tragic accident. The housekeeper's sixteen-year-old son was found drowned in the well. Mr Heath moved to Congleton initially and then bought a bungalow at Grange Road Biddulph. Greenway Bank Hall was empty after that. He died in December 1971. I think it was his request to be in an unmarked grave.

Greenway Bank and the farm 1972. The greenhouses can be seen in the centre (the top car park is there now) and the croquet lawn is at the top of the photo behind the farm.

Knypersley Pool - Gordon Lomas

In 1783 the proprietors of the Grand Trunk Canal Co. decided to cut a 15-mile arm from Shelton to Cauldon and to feed it with a number of reservoirs. The surveyors decided to site the waters amid picturesque scenery and in 1783 30 acres were created to form the 'Serpentine'. When parliamentary sanction was obtained to cut the second Harecastle tunnel they were allowed to increase the water supply and a further 50 acres was formed in 1823, as Knypersley Pool. Various legal restrictions safeguarded the interests of millers and the waters were allowed to flow over a waterfall to Knypersley mill, a stone-built corn grinding mill erected in 1827 with three spacious floors and three pairs of grinding stones, powered by a 14ft overshot water wheel.

The old stone bridge, replaced in 1930.

The original roadway over the reservoir overflow was a stone arch bridge and carried the horse-drawn carriages on their way up Judgefield Lane to Brown Edge and Leek. The steel girder bridge was erected in 1930 and was necessary to carry heavy lorries and the odd passenger coach. Just over the bridge are two properties occupying a pretty position, with good views across the pool and along the road from Greenway Bank, known as Pool Dam Cottages. In 1919 they were part of Biddulph Estates, with one cottage in the occupation of Mrs Farren who lived rent free, and the other let to Mr Daniel Bailey at £7-3s per annum on monthly tenancy with the tenant paying the rates.

The large boulder reputed to be over 20,000 years old and of glacial origin was a familiar object by the side of the pool just before the stone bridge, at the tower end. In 1962 it disappeared overnight without explanation and this brought about numerous stories as to where it came from. One theory was that it was dug from the bed of the pool when the lake was formed. Another was that it appeared when a witch was flying over with her brood in her apron, one fell and on reaching the ground turned into stone. From this story it became known as the 'wishing stone of Knypersley pool'. The North Staffs Aqua Club proved that the witch had not returned to collect it by diving 15ft below the surface where they could touch the boulder. In 1975, 13 years after its disappearance, the dry summer resulted in a rare scene at the lake, when a large expanse of the 50 acres was exposed for the first time in many years. The stone lay firmly planted on the bed. It now stands on the stone bridge near the tower.

Over the stone bridge and elevated above the pathway is a miniature sandstone castle, which originally contained four rooms, once a cold home for some poor estate resident. It is known as the Warders Tower and along with the stone bridge was designed by James Trubshaw in 1828 for Mr James Bateman of Biddulph Grange. From this elevated position the gamekeepers could watch over the wild ducks and snipe in the water as well as deer in the park. A leat, or watercourse, from the pool, was made to flow around the tower to represent a moat.

Behind the tower and approached from a pathway is Gawton's Well, another feature with fascinating yarns associated with it. An 18th century hermit named Gawton is said to have cured himself of the plague by bathing in the waters of the well. It was the only supply of water for the Warders Towers and the three cottages at Lodge Barn. The fields

The Warder's Tower. The last residents were the Hancock family c1956.

around the lake are part of the 146 acre Greenway Bank Farm, which in the days of Mr John Bailey Senior and his sons, became an important dairying and stock rearing, farm. It has been in the Bailey family for around 100 years and today is farmed by Mr Bailey's grandson, Robert.

Opposite the driveway to the farm was a pathway leading to the labourer's dwelling known as Dallows Cottage. The cottage was demolished and the pathway has disappeared.

The Greenway Bank Estate, once owned by the Heath family, was purchased in 1973 by the Staffordshire Council and is now a pleasant country park, allowing visitors to explore the two lakes by constructed pathways and helpful signs. Gone are the days when crowds gathered at Easter-time to enjoy the beauty of the lake and its surrounding countryside, with swing-boats, fairground rides, ice cream and mineral waters as the main attractions.

The bridge and Pool Dam Cottages.

Beryl Dakin

In 1966 I came to Brown Edge, naive of village life and never dreaming that I would settle in the village. I was surprised - the people were lovely. I'd come from Middleport Post Office which I'd done for 13 years.

As time went on I made a lot of friends, had good staff and enjoyed my time. My assistant Jill came with me from Middleport and she was a lovely girl, we got on well, we worked together a long time. Barbara Webb and Marion Fenton did a bit of part-time work for me over the years. Hilda Proctor was a very good friend and she became my daughter's mother-in-law. She helped a bit on the shop side and liked a chat with the customers. Elizabeth Lawton worked part-time for me for about 15 years - a real friend (I want that putting in)

We took over the shop from Mr and Mrs Follows who were retiring. There had been a robbery at the Post Office and it had upset them. The robber lived on the village but came from Durham originally and unfortunately they opened the door to him. He went to prison.

Mr Lay was the policeman then and I hadn't been there above 2 or 3 days when he knocked on the window and he said *'I'm your local bobby and I'll have a look in your shop window at night.'* It was nice to know we had a local bobby but after about 3 years it altered.

We enjoyed village life and everybody was friendly. They all knew if someone was poorly and we cared. I was glad I had the experience of being in Brown Edge. There were quite a few Polish people on the village and they were very nice. My daughter, Derith, went to Endon School, Philip Durber was the headmaster then and all the village children really respected him.

I met characters like Mr Worthy with his goat. We had some fencing at the front and he used to tie the goat up. One morning he was talking to Mrs Brown and she was asking him how he was and while she was talking the goat ate the buttons off her coat. We had a good laugh but Mrs Brown didn't think it was funny! Mr Rastall, the vicar, was a real gentleman. He came in once and Mr Worthy said to him *'Ere I've had such a job getting down this ere bank. Do you think you could give us a lift back, vicar?'* The vicar said *'I don't mind but what about the goat?'* Mr Worthy replied *'We can tie him to the bumper bar and go slow.'*

Harvey Durber was another character. He used to bring my husband comfrey and watercress. He would come in with a bag of field mushrooms as well. Some of the customers brought in tomatoes, runner beans and fresh laid eggs. People were very good.

We moved into the shop in October and that first Christmas was very hectic. We decided we needed a bigger shop so I got a local builder, Johnny Shenton and his father, to extend the premises and the private part of the house, which we liked so much.

We knew all the postmen and deliveries were always made at the same time, twice daily. There was Ralph, Sid, Brian and Frank. We used to see the miner's bus every morning at 6 o'clock - that's all gone. My assistant, Jill, always went home on the bus at the same time and all the Turner's bus men used to shout *'Are you ready Jill?'* Reps. used to call and have a cup of tea. We made time for people - life now is far faster and people don't seem to have time to spare.

We did everything in our head in those days. There were dog licences and fishing licences and a lot of postal orders. We paid out a lot of pensions then but I always felt safe there because we had an Alsatian dog. The dog knew more or less who were customers and who were strangers.

My husband Sam made shelves for wool as there was home knitting done then and we did quite well with it, but of course things die out and changes take place. By then Sam had his own separate business called Fashion Wise. I retired in 1990 and Howard and Teresa Jones took over.

Long service presentation to the post lady Polly Bourne late 1940s. Standing: Rev Ramsden, George Bond, ?, Mr Winkle (Postmaster), Mrs Winkle. Sitting: ?, ?, Harry Proctor, Polly Bourne, ?, ?.

A group in front of the Post Office in the late 1950s, before the extension was added. The postmaster was Mr Follows.

John Basnett - Harrison's Butchers

My brother Alan and I were the seventh generation of butchers in our family. My great grandfather, Enoch Harrison, was born at Ipstones in 1875. His father, Smith Harrison, was a butcher but later became innkeeper at Bottomhouse, which is where he died. Smith's father was Solomon Harrison, born in 1804 and his grandfather was Samuel Harrison, who was born in 1765 - all butchers.

John's great grandfather, Enoch Harrison.

Enoch had a butcher's shop at 1 Clerk Bank in Leek, near to the church. In 1901 he married Hannah Haywood of Brown Edge. She worked in service as a cook for the Nicholson family at Highfield Hall. She lived in at Bridge House with the other servants, not far from Enoch's shop and she probably met him whilst buying meat for the household.

Enoch and his wife, Hannah (née Haywood)

The same year Enoch opened a butcher's shop next to the Lump of Coal public house , which we believe he rented. He also worked as a coal carter at Norton Colliery. His son, Leslie (my grandfather) was born in 1902 and later, in 1904, there was a daughter Dora.

The family later moved into the cottage at the bottom of Hough Hill, called Hough Cottage, where Tom Johnson now lives, which was a grocer's shop owned by Reuben Copeland and before that by Frederick Key. Enoch bought the cottage and also the land below it, and a stable was extended to make a slaughterhouse. Sometime later they took on a stall in Hanley meat market. The meat was taken there by pony and trap at first, then later they bought an Austin straight six, and had the back cut off and converted to carry the meat. It was done in such a way that the cut off body could be bolted back on and the rear seats used. In 1926 Enoch bought a shop with living accommodation in Sandy Lane, which was built by Enoch Dawson.

My Grandfather Leslie married Elsie Brown in 1929. Her older sister, May, was married to Thomas Berrisford, licensee of the Lump of Coal, and she bought Mrs Baddeley's shop which was later taken over by her son, Keith. That same year Leslie bought the bungalow at The Sytch, also built by Enoch Dawson (1927), but didn't move in

Enoch Harrison.

until about 1940 - it was tenanted. The bungalow was built on a piece of land which used to be known as 'Sparrow Park'. Whilst there he had permission off Thomas (Tommy) Powell (he lived opposite, and sold petrol and spare parts) to erect a garage for his car on Tommy's land, near the roadside. When Enoch moved on he gave the garage to Tommy who then used it in place of his old shed.

In 1931 Enoch and Leslie bought a piece of land, about 5 acres from Broad Lane down

John's grandfather Leslie Harrison outside his shop in Sandy Lane.

to Bluestone cottages, known as Brown Bank, off Samuel Willott, a smallholder in Broad Lane. Some of the land was later used as a football field by the local team.

Enoch died in 1933 and Leslie took over the business. In 1943 Les went to an auction at the Plough, at Endon, where he bought Upper and Lower Fernyhough Farms. John Snape was tenant at Upper, and Samuel Hargreaves at Lower. Les moved into Lower in about 1953 and Sid Simcock lived in Upper. Sid started to work for Les after leaving school and Les Lomas was also there at the time. They both went into the forces in 1939 and after the war Sid returned to the shop. He was there until he died in 1977, with some 35 years at the shop.

Leslie and his wife Elsie (née Brown).

Previous to the war Fred Haywood also worked for Enoch and Les. His father, Jack Haywood lived in a caravan behind Bluestone Cottages.

Les's sister, Dora, married George Miller, a butcher in Smallthorne. Les and his wife, Elsie, had 3 daughters - Barbara, Ann and Janet. They all did a bit in the shop and they all married butchers: Ann married Harry Meakin of Meakins & Sons; Janet married Andrew Bould of Knowles (later AN & JM Bould) and my mother, Barbara, married my father, Ken Basnett, who worked at Bratt's butchers, Brown Edge. After their marriage Dad took over the market stall in Hanley. Mum and Dad had 4 children - me, Alan, Kay and Lesley.

Dad's father was Bill Basnett and he moved to Brown Edge from Milton. He was a gardener and served on the parish council and a member of the Working Men's Club. His wife, Martha was a Mountford before she was married and was sister to Harriet Bratt, Sammy Bratt's wife.

My grandfather Les died in 1989 at the age of 87. Mum had taken over the running of the shop when he retired. I worked there for a while and my brother, Alan. The shop closed in July 1994 and re-opened as a chip shop.

George Proctor - by grand-daughter Diane Bond.

Have you noticed the Brittany style cottage, with laughing gargoyles, to your left as you come up High Lane into Brown Edge (the old toll road from Burslem to Leek)? This is Bank End Cottage or 'Laughing Cottage' and our grandfather, George Proctor, rented it from Lord Norton in 1886, when he relocated from Horton. There he lived with his wife, Florence Mayer, who came from Norton Green, and raised 11 children.

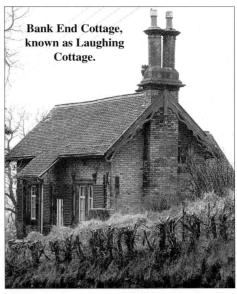

Bank End Cottage, known as Laughing Cottage.

George Proctor worked at the local mine, Bellerton, becoming an overseer while running the farm. Life was scrupulously enterprising and disciplined and the homestead was run efficiently by timetable. Children were: Gertrude (married Jim Beech), George Alan (m. Annie Mayer), Jessie (m. Arthur Mayer), James (m. Edith Stubbs), Lissie (m. Clifford Brown), Fred (died at 20 after accident), Jack (m. Nancy Proctor), Barry (m. Mary Ann Jolley), Winifred Mary (m. William Titley), Madge (m. George Bond) and Florence (called Betty died at 18).

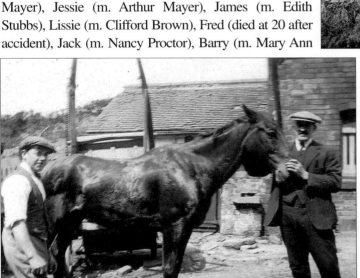

Two sons of George and Florence Proctor, Barry (left) and George Alan.

Our grandmother, Florence, died aged 50, two years after Betty was born. Bovine tuberculosis was a blight then, also taking the life of Betty. Gertrude became a second mother to the family, especially the younger children.

George Proctor offered each of his children the opportunity to further their education beyond

Three more of the children, Winnie, Jack and James c1920.

Leek Westwood or Hanley High School. The nine remaining children became trained school teachers, farmers and mining engineers (with various specialities).

Grandfather George Proctor strongly believed in 'bricks and mortar' and 'you can't make land'. In 1910 he purchased at auction Lot 19, 5 cottages for £260 on Foundry

Square, Norton Green, from the Norton-in-the-Moors Estate. Another time he purchased three houses on Duke Bank Terrace, Norton. His dictates have influenced us in our lives, as did all that we learned from the rather individualistic and strong-minded yet real human beings he fathered.

Five of George's daughters. Gertie at back. Centre: Lissie, Betty. Front: Winifred Mary & Madge.

Aunts, uncles and many cousins surrounded our growing up on High Lane, also the second cousins from second uncles and aunts - the offspring of George's brother, John William Proctor, lower down the lane. Proctors enveloped us - as did ladysmocks, bluebells, buttercups and marsh marigolds, not forgetting hot buttered scones and dripping toast.

BELOW: Brown Edge Church Fete 1945. The queen is Joan Proctor.
Standing: Nora Proctor, Billy Tomkinson, John Proctor, Janet Proctor, Joan, Jim Proctor, Norman Hollins, Graham Mitchell, Joyce Bond, ? Moss. Front: ? Santrian, Pauline Tomkinson, John Fenton. Jim, Joan and John Proctor were triplets, their parents were Barry and Mary Ann Proctor. They were the first triplets born in N.Staffs for 50years. Their mother received the last Bounty (£3) bestowed by the proclaimed King Edward VIII.

Brown Edge Church Fete 1915 probably at Rock Cottage. Centre is the queen, Madge Proctor.